FOR THE CHILDREN

WITH LOVE

Publisher's Note

There is no braver act than honesty. Honesty is love in action, yet it can be a destructive kind of process, facing the harder truths of ourselves and the world around us. So, should you start to struggle in any way, please seek the appropriate help. This book is sold with the understanding that the publisher is not engaged in rendering psychological, financial, legal, or other professional aid. Neither the author nor the publisher shall be liable or responsible for any loss or damage allegedly arising from any information or suggestion contained within this book. With that said, we wish you all the best for this journey you take with yourself and do hope that you reach for help when you become aware that you are in need of it.

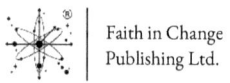

Faith in Change
Publishing Ltd.

Copyright © Ana Maria Santuario 2022. First Edition.

Ana Maria Santuario has asserted her right under the Copyright,
Designs and Patents Act, 1988, to be identified as the author of this work.

Published by: Faith in Change Publishing Ltd
London, England, United Kingdom
www.faithinchange.com

ISBN 978-1-8380743-8-8 (hardback)
ISBN 978-1-8380743-3-3 (paperback)
ISBN 978-1-8380743-4-0 (ebook)
ISBN 978-1-8380743-5-7 (large text edition)
ISBN 978-1-8380743-6-4 (audio book)

Typeset in 11/16pt EB Garamond by Georg Duffner, Vienna, Austria
Graphics Design by Vanessa Steinbeck, London, England, UK
Printed and bound by Ingram Content Group, Global Distributors

All rights reserved. No part of this book may be reproduced or used in any manner
without written permission of the copyright owner, except for use of
quotations in a book review or other purposeful writings.

FAITH

In Stories That Change

Written By
ANA MARIA SANTUARIO

Contents

PREFACE.. 1
STORIES THAT CHANGE 11
LET'S PLAY CATCH UP 23
THE CONTEXT OF SELF 33
THE PHYSICAL BODY,
JUST A LITTLE STARDUST 43
THE FLOW OF THINGS... 51
CONNECTION.. 61
80% WATER, REALLY? 69
TIME TICKS ON,
ALWAYS AND FOREVER 81
PROTECTING OUR YOUNG 93
TOGETHERNESS 107
LETTING GO 119
CHANGE.. 133
THE ILLUSION OF CHOICE................................. 147
BE AWARE, BE VERY AWARE! 163
THE VOICES OF CHILDREN............................... 173
WHAT DO THEY SAY?... 189
THE BASIC NEEDS... 201
CAN WE STOP NOW?.. 213

Preface

A meandering waltz through time and space, we begin to pick apart what it means to be human. We dissect and decode the ways in which we are programmed to present as this individual self and are asked to embrace the notion of change. In ignorance we dwell no longer, as we learn to harness The Revolution of Knowledge that we find ourselves experiencing as a species. If new and different call you forth into the unknown, then I invite you to join me in untangling yourself from the world, as it seems timely for the human collective to slowly begin defining exactly what it is that we are, and to start admitting more to the truth of ourselves. It is time for a wake-up call and what better alarm bell to ring than that of reality?

Our species is made up of stories, we are defined as well as contained by them, and somewhat scared of letting them go. Our identities are entangled by what we think we know, so really, what we are scared of is a loss of our egoic selves, not the silly and often harmful stories that we cling to. Herein, we slowly uncover the truth of who you are and who there is still a chance to become. I do not talk here about improving yourself, much better to accept yourself and embrace the full, whole and colourful human that you were born to be. We must stop living in fear of our own humanness, we must stop smothering the truth of ourselves in shame and denial if we are to move forwards as a humanity. We are all a bit fudged up, can we just let that be okay now?

It is the wellness of our children that concerns me the most, what their futures look like, what their prospects are for a happy life lived well and expansively. With a matrix of information available at the touch of a fingertip, it is time to start discerning the truth from the lies if our children are to have any chance at surviving this mad house they are soon to inherit. I spent a long time delving into the past to make way for a better future for myself, and now I'd like to share what I found with the rest of the world... FAITH.

Before we dive into the thick of it, I will invite you to read a poem intended to slowly align yourself with the ways in which we will be moving forwards herein; to prepare you for looking inwards, based on what you might come to observe in the mirrors of self you will be presented with. To find your way toward Truth, you must first dispel the clouds of

PREFACE

lie and illusion that are fogging up your mind's eye and have you seeing the world as anything less than what it is... A loving gift of Grace, here for us to enjoy, share, and find gratitude in for its wonders. Life is the miracle we're all searching for and I hope that this book will bring you all a little closer to finding a sense of gratitude, whilst helping our children learn to live with it from the get-go.

Gratitude is a speedy cure for all things untrue in this world, including one's own sense of suffering and any lingering longing for a reality different to one's own. It is the bravest thing in the world, to face one's reality, and even braver still to support one's own child in doing so; for you are a fixture of that reality and in turn, you must allow them to recognise the truth of what you are, which can be a scary thing indeed. Please read on to enjoy the aptly placed poem... *Don't Be Scared*...

FAITH

Don't be scared dear ones,
Welcome the thought of change.
Open up your minds and hearts,
To the idea of a New Age.

It is with children in mind that I speak,
With their health and wellbeing at heart.
In light of how disconnected we've come to be,
How far from the truth we're seemingly apart.

There is no answer I can provide,
To ease your discomfort, sorrow or pain.
There is no trick, no miracle pill,
Nothing to justify, reason or name.

I have no god to offer you,
No deity in your faith to place.
I simply offer a mirror,
To look in and see your own grace.

The world presents our reflection,
It tells us every lie we ever believed.
And I found the only point to place my faith,
Was toward the light that I found within me.

PREFACE

The very same light exists,
In all of us, it's true.
But what prevents us from seeing it,
Except the illusions they've sold to you?

Do you know that you're beautiful?
Do you know you're made up of stars?
Do you wander around in awe,
With the truth of yourself in your heart?

There is no way to know,
What is right from wrong.
Other than to feel your way,
Toward the stories that truly belong.

All that doesn't belong creates conflict,
Inside of yourself is where it exists.
Only words spoken aloud become real,
As your distaste with reality permeates and persists.

What do you spend your time talking about?
Is it a jolly good waste of time?
Or do you sit and treasure each moment,
That shall never again be yours, nor mine?

FAITH

Time is something we'll never stop,
Nor catch as a fleeting thought.
Can you start to ask yourself,
In which part of the past you are caught?

Does the story you're telling even belong to you?
Or to another time and place?
Are the thoughts you're believing even relevant,
Or are your judgments totally misplaced?

Stop treating the world as your enemy,
Come to see it as a mirror instead.
One to reflect back all the lie and illusion,
That exists only in your own head.

It is time to stop believing,
In regurgitated and manipulated truths.
And shift more to the heart of who we ought to be,
If we only believed that we could.

The truth is, it's too late for us,
Our way of programming is all set.
Like computers hardwired to process and react,
According to the wiring in our own head.

But *our* children, now they have a fighting chance,
At becoming what we cannot.
Healthy, happy, contented humans,
Comfortable and accepting of their lot.

Gratitude is the answer to most of our strife,
When our greed is balanced in kind.
Our intrinsic fear of not enough,
Is but an ancestral fear of our collective mind.

There is no need to fear The Other,
Not any longer and never more.
If we are brave enough to face the past,
And finally close its door.

We now know more than any other,
Conscious beings that we so are.
And as knowledge evolves, so too do we,
For already we've come so far.

But when do we say, 'Enough now!'
When do we stop wasting our time?
Repeating conflict belonging to the past,
Never neither yours, nor mine?

FAITH

These stories that separate, they are not ours,
They never were and never shall be.
Can we let the light of children shine as truth,
And let them become what we were meant to be?

Can we prepare them for a world that doesn't love,
And teach them to love themselves?
For this is the thing we all need to survive,
The battle in which we find ourselves.

The world has taken you hostage,
Filled you up with things untrue.
It told you that you should be scared of me,
And I, in turn, of you.

This fear is how they control you,
Who are *they*, I'll never know.
But I do know the fear they create and sustain,
Is what prevents the world from becoming whole.

Whole people is what will make the world whole,
Healed, healthy, happy individuals are key.
And I'm sorry to break it to you buddy,
But it's too late for you and me.

However, we still have a chance to save the kids,
We have a chance to set them free.
If we have the courage to face the truth,
By looking at you, and realizing, you're just like me.

CHAPTER 1

Stories That Change

Stories are what shape us, they are an imprint of time and space that live on in our body and mind. Every single story lived becomes this you, this self, this ego structure of thought, feeling, emotion and sensation. You are your stories and your stories are you. Can you sit with that for a moment?

You are your stories. Your stories are you.

Each one of us has lived a totally unique sequence of events, everything will have been individualized, from each breath of air breathed, to the mouthfuls of food eaten, to the place, position and people we were born to. Then there's the family home, that crazy zone full of the only people who really know you, yet don't know you at the same time, and it is all of these experiences combined that come to result in this beautiful and incredible you.

No one has ever known me because no one has ever known my stories. Stories are what connect people and my stories always seemed inconsequential to others, no one has ever really listened to me, not really. I did pay a therapist for a year and half to listen to my woes. However, as time went on and my stories of trauma left me, the ones that no one wanted to hear, but the very ones that stood in the way of me telling the other stories of myself and my life, well, I became utterly depressed by the realization that my therapist was my best friend. I was horrified when I realized that a man whom I paid to listen to me for one hour a week was my closest ally in life.

However, when I sat with perspective and looked back over a life veiled in trauma and shame, a life hidden in the shadows of experience, a life spent watching other people connect, well, I figured that sitting there with that therapist was perhaps the bravest thing I could have ever done. And with that, I let go of my lingering shame and allowed him to remain my mate for another six months, accepting that life was exactly as it needed to be. Acceptance. A big word. A loaded word. It calls on one to become a better person, it calls on one to take in the bigger picture of life. It also calls on a person to step into the wonder of the moment that is *now*. When you accept, you sit still with your body and mind and allow all that arises to pass, be it good or bad, light or dark. We lie about who we are. For the most part this is true, everyone is lying to themselves, about themselves, about the life they are living, because the truth is scary.

Teenagers see this clearer than anyone, perhaps that's why they are so angry a lot of the time, because they look around at all of these adults telling them how to live life, yet they don't see many adults living an existence they would aspire to mimic. You know, let's cut through the ego-protective layer of crap that anything is right about the world. Do you know what I know? I was not born to this earth of potential adventure, wonder and awe to follow the rules and ways of others and do what I'm told forever, especially if those others have no sense of joy about them. Let joy be your radar folks, listen to no one in misery or pain, listen to those who have found joy, for they have walked a path worth learning from.

We live in a world overstimulated by and desensitized to pain and suffering, which means we think that it's normal. Well, I'm here to tell you that it's not! Nothing about the way we live as human animals is normal, we are so far removed from our natural way of being that it has become something to be debated. Just take a look at the word *diet*, how many stories live in your body and mind that are attached to that one word? Too many to count, right? Earlier I referred to acceptance as a big word, but so too is the word, *diet*. This one word triggers a whole array of thoughts, feelings, urges and impulses within everyone. So how did these 'components of self' come to be there? How did this combination of beliefs, opinions, judgements and 'knowledge' come to live inside of you and therefore determine particular patterns and cycles of your day-to-day existence?

Before we go into dissecting the stories that make us, we first need to understand how they came to be a part of us and how they influence our somewhat auto-piloted existence. From birth we are subjected to an onslaught of sensory experiences, none of which we choose, very few of which are consciously chosen for us. We are born to this earth a tiny, vulnerable, squirming little animal, full of needs that require meeting, with too many parents ignorant to their own ignorance. Is it a fear of failure that keeps parents from expanding their knowledge, too scared as they are, be it consciously or subconsciously, that they have gotten it so undeniably wrong? Do they worry that they've messed their kids up in some irreversible way, so it becomes easier to avoid the topic altogether and simply smother the situation in denial and shame, pretending all is fine? Or did they simply receive nothing that looked like love themselves as a child, and so have zero reference as to how to bestow it upon their own offspring?

Love begets love, and parents are like computer chips, ready to install patterns, stories and beliefs into their children. What are you uploading them with? Now that is a great question to ponder, even before any planned conception, especially since it may highlight that you've got some self-work to do before harming a child by simply being who and what you presently are. These are the harder truths, but of no less value than the knowing that when your decision is to feed your child with nutritious homemade meals, their inward world will become much healthier than a body fed with processed, greasy and fatty foods. Healthy love is what our young need, now more than ever, and it is a thing to be learned, cultivated and bestowed; not necessarily *given*, because love is a thing to become, not really to give and to take.

Love begets love, an important thing to ponder as we move on... Especially since it's sad to see how many people tick on pretending everything is fine. You know, quite a lot of the time life is not okay, another thing that teenagers are very aware of, yet another story they are told they've gotten wrong. Why? Because the adults are right, always. End of. Funnily enough, even when proven wrong with reason, logic and doubt, they still find themselves pulling the long

FAITH

straw of an argument at times. I have always found age a weird thing to measure wisdom by in truth, because I have heard the most ignorant and ill-informed words come out of a pensioner's mouth, and the truest of wisdom blurted out by a three-year-old.

I think back to a conversation with my friend's son, Jessiah, in reference to the veggie garden my friend Kasim ensures he grows with his sons every summer (shout out to Marley, both boys need their names on this page). Kasim lives in Montserrat, and being a native Caribbean Rasta he inherited particular mindsets towards nature and food, consequently, these staples of life are cherished and talked about. My brother from another mother connects the dots of existence for his boys and lets them watch the magic of life grow and transform before their eyes. What a wonderful mirror nature presents for our own journeys:

Me: *Jessiah, I heard you're growing some strawberries?*
Jessiah (in an absolutely incredulous tone): *I am not! They're growing themselves.*
Me: *Far out, Little Dude! Yes, they are. Yes. They. Are.*

My tiny friend's words still vibrate through me today and they remain some of the wisest I've ever heard spoken aloud. I believe that so much wisdom is to be found in innocence, less so in the learned man and woman. Knowledge vs. wisdom, an interesting debate for philosophers. I, however, decided that I reserve the right to choose what I think for myself; it seems everyone else does, it's just that not enough people *think* about what they think. I'd like to look at how that conversation might go with an adult, let's call him Stuart:

Me: *Hey Stu, I heard you've been growing some strawberries?*
Stuart: *Oh yeah, they're delicious, much juicier than the ones I grew last year. I prepared a better mulch this time. And check these out, the blueberries are ripening too. Green fingers award, here I come!*
Me: *Nice one. May I try one, please?*

An equally pleasant conversation, but of a less mind-blowing nature. You see, Stuart has adopted the false belief that the growth of the strawberries is his own personal achievement, that he is somehow responsible for their very nature, to grow, flower and fruit. If he were smart, he'd realize wholeheartedly that he might offer nutrients to this living entity, he might monitor and maintain a consistent environment, but he has nothing to do with the fact that they grow or even exist.

As much can be said for children. I watch adults pride

FAITH

themselves on their offspring, on the fact that they have reproduced a tiny human and care for its basic needs, despite not even doing that well half of the time. But let's get this straight, there is no miracle in birth, it happens over a million times a week all over the world. *Life* is the common miracle, and we live this miracle every single day, yet we are born having forgotten it and there are very few people around to remind us. That miraculous energy of a newborn baby, the glow of joy and love they spread through a room, this is the essence of life's energy being felt, not simply a collective nod to the 'miracle of birth.'

The world is changing.
And why is it changing?
Because what we know is changing.

Knowledge is power. Knowledge is change. Knowledge is an ever-evolving entity fuelled by the minds of humankind. I once met a man in the Swiss Alps, Silvio, a sculptor of stone and maker of music. He would make large, musical, stone xylophones, which, when played, would emit deep vibrations, sometimes sounding like the call of an orca, and take them to do vibrational work with children in local schools. He also loved playing with words, dissecting their origins and presenting delectable nuggets of contemplation.

He once said to me, as we sat around a friend's kitchen table, 'Knowledge, it has no-ledge.'

It took me years to gain clarity with regard to these words that lingered. For me, the words that stick always require revisits and revisions until they make sense, they are like a riddle that needs to be solved and it wasn't until recently that I understood what the words meant to me. You see, I've been searching for something all of my life, call it what you will, a quest for meaning, a longing for a deeper purpose, a lost soul wandering aimlessly for its calling. Yet, it was none of these things that drove my thirst for a variety of lived experience and knowledge, it was a deep knowing I'd had since a young age that no adults around me seemed to have a clue what they were talking about. No one had the knowledge I was seeking, perhaps that which might bring a sense of peace and purpose. Not one person I observed was living a life that I aspired to live, and something just felt very off about it all.

Now, as I've grown and matured, gained perspective and forgiven my elders for their perceived failures, I can see that they did not fail at all, they simply didn't know what I know; they were programmed with different thoughts, beliefs and behaviours. Different 'knowledge'. They were trapped in a past that was not my own, which does not put them at fault, it simply makes them human. Isn't it the way of things, to reluctantly repeat the ways of our elders? Does this not shine a new light on the so-called *teenage rebellion*, when our young seem so convinced that we're wrong about things, yet they remain brave and bold enough to tell us so, as well as naïve enough to consider that they might possibly win the war they wage against adulthood? But mightn't the teens be right and it be the adults who're wrong? Weren't we once also those righteous teens, living the same tumultuous transition into adulthood, unable to even fathom the notion of our lives replicating that of our parents'? However, don't most of us eventually succumb to some compromised existence, one which our younger selves would perhaps give us a slap for sitting still and accepting?

So, is it time for us, as a collective group of informed and learned grown-ups, to admit more to the truth of our human ways and help free our young from them? Is it time to admit that every single collective, society and nation throughout history has considered themselves right about certain things, things that have later come to be dispelled or disproven? Although, it's important to note that things are never merely disproven, I prefer to say that they are developed or built upon, like a complex structure, with every brick, screw and nail there to hold things in place. I imagine our human knowledge to be a bit like a constructional matrix, made up of light, time and space, with every minute particle finding meaning by way of its place in the bigger picture.

It's time to acknowledge that knowledge has *no ledge*, it will evolve, change and transform forever. Those who came before us were determinably wrong about many things, so might we be too? Could we even be so bold as to say that we are most certainly wrong about a heck of a lot? For change and growth to happen we must make space for it to do so. A plant cannot grow in a damp, dark cupboard, it needs space, fertile soil, sunlight and water. Might we too require particular energetic elements as growing individuals? Might we respond well when surrounded by particular vibrations, might our physiological systems decompress and find release in the expressive arts, mightn't physics and chemistry come to inform the way we approach our practices with children? Might an overcrowded and loud classroom for a proportionate period of time in childhood *not* be the best environment within which to learn and become your best self?

We all come to be in much the same manner; be born, live some stuff, learn some stuff, become this utterly unique individual with a label (your name), and let's not forget the final chapter, be dead. This is certainly oversimplifying life into one of the basest of forms, however, it's relatively accurate. And so, if life really is this miracle, if it's all we get,

FAITH

whether it be one or multiple reincarnations, whether there be an afterlife, whether the sky really be blue, what does it matter? I say we get to talking about how to live life well and in order to do that, we must first look at how humans, en masse, came to live it so very poorly.

CHAPTER 2

Let's Play Catch Up

So, let's dive right into the thick of it, you are energy, can we agree on that? Do you know enough about physics and chemistry to inform a shared agreement that you are made up of moving energy? Gone are the days of thinking we are a singular, solid moving object; we are changing, adapting, responding and reacting all of the time. Our bodies are this complex machine, a living breathing organism made up of atoms, molecules, vibrations and frequencies. For some reason we think we're special, though I don't really know why, birds can fly after all, but for the most part, we are a biological animal.

It only takes sitting and watching baby monkeys play, or a lion yawn, to make connections between yourself and other mammals. The similarities between humans and apes both amuse and fascinate me, there is a knowing behind their eyes that lies beyond our comprehension. It intrigues me how humans seem to mostly value the intelligences that they can understand, those they can measure, test and quantify. Humans are ignorant to believe that they truly know anything; nature, the mother of all on earth, all things made up of matter, material and movement, well, she is the sustaining deity of all we live and breathe. Humans, they simply learned to observe, label and manipulate what she birthed and co-created.

Mother Nature's intelligence can be measured by the sustainable harmony and immeasurable beauty of all she birthed. There is no other place more equipped to take you to the space of stillness within than the arms of nature. She envelops you with her soothing bird song, hugs you with the wind and warms your face with the shine of the sun. In contrast, the human's intelligence creates chaos and conflict, a world where so much is believed to be known, yet so very little seems to be understood. I like to think that we, as a humanity, are living two revolutions at once, two revolutions that are symbiotic to one another, The Technological Revolution and The Revolution of Knowledge. *The Tech-Knowledge Revolution*—can I coin that phrase?

For far too long, knowledge has been used as a tool for manipulation, to create false beliefs and fear within the minds and hearts of humankind. It is not too far into the history of man that majority populations were left ignorant and illiterate to the betterment of the few. Heck, there was a time when books were kept under lock and key, written in Latin and only a few were trained to read and 'translate' the very mandates of life. In contrast, we now have the internet and access to knowledge like never before, but how does one begin to syphon off knowledge that is useful from that which is cloaked in false wisdom, the guise of fear incarnate?

Humans are fear-based creatures, let's get that straight. Any other story told and believed in regard to our species is simply born from an inability to admit to the truth of oneself. We begin to be programmed with fear-based beliefs from birth; when we touch something hot, we learn not to do it again; when we perhaps walk in the dark and bump our knee, we then learn to turn a light on or adjust the way we move and extend our hands ahead of us next time. The point is, from the get-go, we explore and adapt to our external environment. Our first sensory explorations as babies involve taste, texture and touch. We see reflections of light that our mind cannot yet classify and comprehend, we hear sounds that are brand new and are received by our physiological systems as such. We know nothing yet. If we look at what it is to know nothing, can we then come to see what we think it means to know something?

FAITH

As a developing infant we do what all young mammals do: we seek safety, food, warmth and comfort. We use our senses to detect and process what our primary carers do, we absorb this as the known and expected way of living life, then we mirror and mimic this as the norm. Having travelled far and wide on this earth, I have come to observe the following to be true: people everywhere think that they're right about their way of life, be it about their belief system, their dietary preferences, choice of music, clothing, or even their job. The fact is, we mostly stumble into the life we live and very few of us choose the trajectory of our lives. We are born to our place and position in life, and from there we develop into this individual human by way of a unique sequence of experiences and events, thus being programmed to express outwardly as this individual *ego* or *self*.

We were told at a young age that it was necessary to define ourselves, to choose a pathway in life and stick with it, for that was a certain road to security and safety. Yet, the options presented to us are incessantly limited by fear. All traditional ways of living life are rooted in ancestral, fear-based, animalistic survival instincts and patterns. Just look at the overwhelming fear that fuels a human's need to secure a house or land. This is a universal truth of humans: we all seek security in shelter. What else is important to all humans? That they can access water, food and hygiene facilities, be it a Western plumbing system or a fresh flowing river. The basic needs of humans are the one consistent element of life across the globe. But rather than enjoying creating and sustaining the home in all of its beautiful necessity, we live in constant fear that it's going to disappear somehow, never certain of our own security. Sadly, this will be the reality for many humans on earth, yet it is by acknowledging this fact that I came to this very simple truth:

If you, in this moment, have a secure and safe shelter, as well as ease of access to food and water, then you can consider yourself a lucky human. If you have anything in excess of this, well, consider yourself privileged.

The modern world feeds on ingrained human programming rooted in primal survival instinct. The consumerist market feeds on an internal fear that you are not good enough exactly as you are, yet it is the very monster of illusion that breathes life into the birth of the fear in the first place. For many of us in the Western world, we are not born many generations after wartimes, times of austerity and rationing, times of 'not enough.' These people, our ancestors, were our teachers, but they were people born into times when they were justifiably scared of 'The Other.' Yet, the fears that existed in those times no longer belong to this world. Can I tell you a secret? It's one of the best kept...

You are safe now.

The world would have you think you're not, that you must fear what is different or unknown, but the chances are that new and different will only ever enrich your mind, heart and soul. We are so scared of everything: change, new, different, challenge, loss, failure, success, love. My goodness, we are so scared of living life, whilst being simultaneously trapped by the fear of death. It is of course healthy to fear death, to an extent, it is what has a person run from a fire or stay out of crocodile-infested waters. When fear is informed by a measure of reasonable risk then it seems sensical to listen to it. But that same primal reaction that stops you from swimming with crocs is the very same physiological fear that stops you from singing on stage just for the fun of it.

Years ago, I started to watch children in a new way, with an element of wonder about my contemplations, a wonder that led me to ask, *what on earth happens to us all?* We all begin life with sunshine inside of our hearts, we sing, dance and play, we gasp at the beauty of a rainbow and welcome the rain on our face. We laugh, we forgive, we love unconditionally. However, somewhere along the way we learn to believe other things, things the adults around us model and teach. In other words, we learn to fear.

Let's go back to that little baby exploring the world at its own pace, allowed to make choices based on its own lived experience. If it does not like a certain food or flavour then it will decidedly spit out said food and demand an alternative. However, once a child can communicate, well, it can begin to be conditioned and trained. I wonder at what age it is that parents begin to talk their children into eating the food on offer and stop allowing the child the privilege of choice and refusal.

It's strange to observe the various eating habits of children across the world. From what I see, it is the story of value placed on the food that determines the child's relationship with it. There's a big difference between telling a child that they must eat their greens because you said so, and explaining the nature of connection between the food and the very energy we need to live and thrive as human beings. In most religions a moment of grace is taken in gratitude for food, for the blessing of a full belly. Intrigued by humans and their various ways of living life, I find it unavoidable to draw several connections between the belief systems that exist around the world.

All of them are sustained by the belief that there is a creator of sorts, a deity, a greater power that exists beyond reason or logic. All require Faith, a five-letter word that holds the whole world together. I just think it's funny how everybody seems to be telling a different story about the same thing, yet they remain in constant conflict about the way it is told. These stories are from other times and places, they belong to different societies and collectives. Stories are always changing, right alongside humans. Once upon a time, the ancient Egyptians believed in the Sun God Ra and an afterlife paid for in treasure. Over time, power shifts perhaps meant that the human powers-that-be needed to find a way to enable the masses a right to a beautiful afterlife too, there be born a heaven for all. Hell was of course needed to ensure that an intrinsic fear of death be sustained.

Fear, the one and only thing that keeps humans divided and out of love. Fear of the other. Fear of the threat of different. Fear of change for fear of being wrong. Fear of wrongness threatening the tidy little package of meaning attached to your life. Fear of reality. Reality isn't something we talk about much, is it? I think perhaps because the language for it has not existed, or at least hasn't been universally accepted enough to move beyond mathematical equation and representation.

You are energy in motion.

The stories of the past refer to you as a mind, body and soul. This was a story told within the realms of the knowledge and understanding accessible at the time. Since the evolution of humankind and its stories propelled at a rate that has not yet been lived by our species, it seems to me that we need to wake up and catch up. As a living mix of cultures and generations, we need to learn how to drop stories that don't belong in the here and now, we need to let go of conflicting nonsense rooted in a history of poor education and limited experience. We need to let go of our fear of being wrong and see the utter wisdom and grace found in admitting you're not quite sure about something.

It's understandable, you know, to be afraid, it's just important to understand where that fear comes from. You see, you are born to a world built around concepts such as right and wrong; failure and success; good and bad; positive and negative; and most experiences that we live are classified as such within our bodies and minds. We then go on to subconsciously base our choices on whether the experience previously lived was pleasant or unpleasant overall. And what determines whether an experience is pleasant or unpleasant? How your body and mind react to it, that's all.

CHAPTER 3

The Context of Self

So, what does, 'You are energy in motion,' mean when applied within the context of the self? It's a term thrown around a lot, sometimes as though these are magical words that should break some spell, perhaps the spell of the illusion of your own mundaneness. You are made up of the same stuff as stars after all, and when we look up at a night sky twinkling with travelling light, we are inspired with wonder and awe. For a moment our mind sits on the edge of not knowing, that feeling perhaps young infants have when they first gaze upon things with a recognition of their existence, yet no comprehension of their perceived and attached meaning.

I wonder why we never gaze in the mirror at the majesty of our own existence. I mean, what were the chances of your existence as this individual you? What were the chances of that exact egg and sperm coming together? The chances of you existing in this infinite universe are, well, infinite. Infinity, another fabulous word to sit with and boggle your own mind. Can any human mind grasp the concept of infinity, of foreverness? Our minds measure in time and quantify meaning by use of language, be it lexical or mathematical. The mind can visualize both the real and imagined, it can create representations of things not found within reality, such as unicorns, pixies and mermaids. How did such images and creatures come to exist within the mind of humankind?

The mind. For me, this is a word as equally incomprehensible as infinity. How can a mind know itself? How can a mind know what it is? Can you see your own mind? Can you hear it? Can you ever control what it thinks, how it reacts or how it determines any subsequent actions? In my opinion, the answer is no, but we'll get to that later. You can be aware of its existence and hone this self-awareness with training and practice, but I just cannot see how it'll ever be possible to define the mind within itself. If the mind creates the words and stories, surely, it's beyond its own definition?

Then there's the body, the physical you, the one made up of 3D matter and material, this supercomputer that runs all by itself without any instruction manual, all it needs is a little fuel in the form of the right nutrients, vitamins and minerals. Just as a car needs oil to energize action and movement, the only real reason for eating and drinking is to fuel the vessel you use to navigate your way through life. But sadly, even a concept as natural as dietary requirements has become a maze of misinformation, resulting in nothing but a lack of trust in your own body to know exactly what it needs. And how does this happen?

> *The world fudges with your mind,*
> *that elusive thing that we know exists,*
> *but learn very little about.*

With all the information in the world I do wonder why the education system still resembles Victorian principles. It is my opinion that in this day and age of sensory overload, mass manipulation and brainwashing, it is our responsibility as adults to teach children and young people about themselves. About how their mind is vulnerable to believing things that are not true because of some perverse, oppressive notion that adults know best and it's important to listen to what they have to say.

You know, even as an adult I must admit that I rarely come across a person worth listening to. Don't get me wrong, I love people, I find them interesting, but what is the *worth* of

FAITH

interesting? I guess it depends who you're talking to and what your interests are, but let me expand on this point before I quickly get labelled as arrogant. I know some amazing musicians, I love to play alongside them and enjoy the vibrational charge of an epic jam sesh, I love to listen to them talk about various artists or songs. It's all very *interesting,* and most certainly holds value as a connected, nurturing and expansive human experience, but I never learn much beyond interesting. Of course, for a band manager this kind of discourse would be highly valued and enrich a key element of their life, so the *worth* of the exchange would be very different.

So, what makes something worth listening to in my book? Well, any lived or learned thing that assists in questioning what you think you already know. I experienced first-hand how learning about oneself can positively impact the trajectory of one's life, and from what I observe it seems safe to say that people operate with a subconscious fear of learning about themselves. You see, that mirror I thought it might be nice to look in earlier, so I might gaze upon my own magical nature, it exists for everyone, the problem lies in the perception of what we see and what that might reveal about our deeper selves. It is the hardest thing in life, to admit to the truth of oneself, truly, any person that commits to self-work and an honest critique of themselves is a warrior

THE CONTEXT OF SELF

of a new kind, one only understood by another of their own nature.

You see, I transformed myself. It's impossible to explain to people who haven't done it, and I've given up trying. I simply decided to just be this new me now and let go of needing to be understood. It's amazing how much conflict is created by the human need to be understood, and even worse, to be right. Too many people think they're right about things only because other people who thought they were right about them told them it was right. The world is built on a cycle of regurgitated stories and beliefs, many of which are fear-based and hold no real worth. My big question is, can we press pause, can we release fear for a moment, fear of being wrong, and open our mind up to the infinite possibility that humans are in fact wrong about everything, just like they were in the past?

I don't for one second claim to be right. There is no right.
That's what I'd like to make fundamentally clear.
No stories are true. No stories hold an answer. No stories are to be believed without some degree of critical digestion.

There is only ever the most current knowledge and understanding to inform our ways of life. And what is knowledge? It is the catalogue of useful information held within your mind-body. Knowledge is the only useful thing, it is what we use to make meaning of the world and expand our comprehension of what it means to be human. There is no finish line in this evolution, not one any of us will live to see anyway. One day, it is our generations that will be analysed and studied within the history books and what a period in time it will be to dissect, in its ever-changing complexity and ever-expanding variety, the modern world is quite simply a mad house.

In my world, history is but a mirror to see the madness of men. We look back to the past with an arrogant superiority, taking in how far we've come like we had some role to play in the naturally occurring phenomenon of the evolution of man. I, for one, am able to admit that I had no part to play in the resulting world today, but I do take credit for speedily waking up to the reality of it. Humans don't see themselves clearly, they don't realize that they are just the same as their ancestors, a semi-blank human computer born to Earth and programmed with subsequent patterns, cycles and stories, which then come to manifest as this individual you. We become this 'self,' walking around with a name, happily counting, year by year, how many times we sit on the earth as it circles the sun, which it will continue to do long after we're gone.

So, let's return to that word now, energy. What does it

mean, what value does it hold when applied to what we know about the self? The answer: it potentially transforms the human experience so that it might be lived with more awareness of the unknown. If you can allow your mind to grasp and then appreciate the concept of yourself as energy in motion, well, you are halfway to heaven. When you accept yourself as an energetic entity, one that is no more separate from the world than a single drop of water is from the ocean, that's when you sit alongside something a little more like truth. The illusions we believe about ourselves and life are merely stories of the past that were told within the realms of accessible knowledge and understanding of different times and places.

Today, so much has changed, it is no longer a tribe facing off against a tribe with slightly different ideologies, the world has become smaller and with it, fear and conflict have grown in intensity, volume and variety. The threat to one's ego and self has multiplied, the threat I speak of is conflicting knowledge and experience, the threat of information that may challenge what you think you know. The ease with which a human mind might dismiss another person's belief system as 'wrong' may just be one of the most hysterical moments a person can live. Basically, one says, the invisible thing I have faith in is real, but yours is totally imagined.

FAITH

But what if neither is real nor unreal? What if humans got it wrong about these doctrines and books? What if humans became disciples when they were supposed to thrive as the co-creators of their own lives? What if these books are all there with one sole purpose, to point you home toward the truth of yourself? What if somewhere along the way we got lost in the maze of rightness and wrongness, we got lost in the words and forgot what we were looking for all along, a feeling of peace, love and joy? Before we move on, may I let you in on another little secret?

It doesn't matter which road you take home;
All paths lead to Love...

I'd like to take an honest moment to express my intrigue at the human ability to deny the existence of another person's god but claim an all-knowing stance on their own. As someone who grew up on the outside of mainstream religion, I was very much left to define and determine my own thoughts and feelings about life, which resulted in me watching people of faith with a curious interest. The devotion to the unknown and unseen, a practice I have seen in every corner of the earth I've visited, was once something I couldn't wrap my mind around. In my early days of travel, I'll admit I was fairly judgmental, fascinated of course, but internally judgmental too. I thought that all of these people devoting their lives to religious practices were believing in the adult equivalent of fairy tales, and to an extent I still do, but only because too many people believe blindly and think too little about how they came to believe in what they do.

However, as I sat down to Hindu chanting and meditation in India, as I was welcomed to Islamic prayer sessions or sat in a church in Malaysia listening to hymns being sung, well, I never did start to believe what they did, fundamentally because I understood nothing of the language, but I did get to *feel* some things. I've cried during the gentle moment of release that meditation provides and felt the vibrational residue linger in my body after a bhajan musical chant in Sanskrit. I've felt the gentle comfort of a community's faith in Allah as it soothes the pain of a shared loss. I've experienced the hug of the unknown as I've sat in a church and listened to a piano and clarinet releasing a soothing melody. Yet, I've also discovered the tranquility of nature and the opportunity it presents to see your own wonder and beauty. A world without man, that's the world I enjoy most. God's world. Not mine.

You see, no one taught me a story about God, and I count myself lucky for that, as it seems I found my own way towards making meaning of this life I am here living. This is what led me to determine that it really doesn't matter what path finds you, just welcome it, surrender, and trust that life will always provide you with a road home to the peace that lies in your own heart. Somewhere along the way we became too reliant on words to point the way and forgot that we should be allowing feeling to inform us to an equal extent. Feelings tell us so much, they let us know when a situation is good for us or if particular people are toxic to our life. The trouble is, we've forgotten how to truly feel; and no wonder, with so much pain, chaos and destruction, it seems an intelligent survival mechanism of our physical body is to desensitize our system so that it too does not succumb to the pain and destruction of the world. Smart body.

CHAPTER 4

The Physical Body, Just a Little Stardust

The body is where feelings happen. We grow up taking the existence of feelings for granted, rarely pausing to consider what they are or why they are there. We accept the spectrum of emotion as a normality of life, but who's to say that we experience anything in the same way as another? In fact, we definitely don't because we will always have our own unique thought patterns occurring as a natural reaction to external stimuli. It is the thought about a thing that determines whether the experience lived is pleasant or unpleasant. And what is a thought, it is a sequence of happenings that result in a lived reaction, perhaps speech, a physical outburst, or simply the turning on of a light switch. Thoughts happen all the time, with or without our knowing, they even happen when we sleep as we see original images and events emerge from our imaginations and be labelled as dreams.

We use these words, these lexical labels, to attach a catalogable meaning to every single 'discovery,' a.k.a., every observable or measurable thing we determine to exist. I have often been amused by the existence of certain words, one like *fork*, I mean, what came first, the fork we eat with or the fork in the road? And who on earth uttered that sound out of their mouth and saw fit to forever condemn the English-speaking world to use it daily in the kitchen? And then there are words like dreams, ocean, love or God, and we accept them with the same passive naivety as when an adult first gets us to mimic back the word, 'fork.' Do you see how stupid we are? We literally are born to this earth and just believe what we're told, unless we're lucky enough to be raised a critical thinker, live an experience that jolts us out of our perceived reality, or are simply born with a mistrust of a world that thinks it knows everything.

It doesn't really matter that we are this way, humanness is what I like to call it when our egos get the better of us, in whatever manner that may occur, be it spite, jealousy, rage, insecurity, judgement or pessimism. It can also manifest as eternal optimism, excitement, kindness, love and joy. The ego is all of these things. The ego is the self and all it combines. And the home of your ego... the body. When you think about it, we are the ugliest apes on the planet, with our bald bodies and funny patches of hair sprouting from strange places. But the thing is, if we were all born with hairy bodies, we'd be none the wiser and fully accept ourselves as the only talking hair-covered primates, whilst still living with the same superior stance over all else.

It is not our bodies that separate us from other animals, physiologically we are much the same, our bodies can even receive aortic valve replacements from pigs and cows, not even our closest genetic relatives are used, those of course being chimpanzees. What separates us is this mind of ours, which can think beyond time and imagine beyond reality. We react differently to the world when compared with other animals, I think we might be scared of it, beyond moments of reasonable fear which are experienced by most living things, we live in perpetual fear of life and truly living it. But why, I'll tell you: this body of ours works so bloody hard to keep us safe from the threats of the world, but it hasn't yet realized that those threats that existed for millennia just don't anymore.

> *What is a fear reaction but a primitive survival mechanism inbuilt into your system, intended to keep you safe and alive?*

Let's not get fear wrong, it's there for a very good reason, it's there to be felt and experienced. It's just, do we actually get what fear is or why it's there, and do we consider that our bodies might be functioning with outdated ancestrally related patterns and reactions? Primitive fear-based survival instincts, that's ultimately what we operate on, unless you're a psychopath, a few of whom I've met, and I can say it's a most fascinating life that is lived without cognitive fear or the softer, emotion-based reactions. Without fear standing in the way a person gets to do exactly what they want whenever they want to do it. Yet we are constrained within the prison cell of our own minds, living a limited life behind bars, occasionally making a run for it before returning to the welcoming arms of familiarity and predictability.

There's nothing wrong with this, like I said, humanness. Let's just stop pretending about it all though, please, for the love of God, can we all stop pretending that life is okay and that we are living it the way it should be lived. Just because the humans before us had to endure a life of basic survival, it doesn't mean that we cannot rise off the back of their perseverance and gracefully thank those who lived before us for surviving this world and working hard to make it what it is today. But my goodness, can we start admitting to the big truths, can we start growing up and owning our place on this earth as someone with a thinking and questioning mind? Can we stop fearing ourselves and the reality of what we are? An animal that thinks a bit, and possibly considers what it thinks as far too important. Can we admit that the humans of the past got us here, but it's up to us to decide which way we go?

So, do we journey bravely towards truth and break down barriers of conflict and strife? Or do we dwell in ignorance and illusion and ignore the elephant in the room? What elephant you might ask? Why, *you* of course. You are the only elephant in the room at any given time, the big grey collection of matter clouding your own way. All of your stories make up that elephant, your judgements, beliefs, opinions and expectations. And where do they live? In your body. This shadow of grey exists only inside of you.

Matter makes up life, it's what you are, it's what you breathe, it's what you wash in and drive to work. Matter makes up all in existence. Why is this important to know? How can it not be? At the beginning of this book I talked about us getting to talking about life and how to live it well, and that first starts with understanding the body, this vessel we are blessed with to house us through life. It's the only true home we have, the rest is decoration. I am not here to write things that have already been written so I do not wish to explain the biology, physics or chemistry of the physical form, neither will I preach any dietary preference or condemn the likes of big pharma and the food industries, that's all out there already, just hit Google. I wish to attempt to tell new stories...

The body is a miracle, is it not?
I mean, the fact that we can stand up with
balance and walk should be impossible, but it isn't.

Why aren't we taught this in school, what a miracle it is to stand and walk, not everybody can after all. The value of things is something that is taught and learned, not blindly absorbed from the ether, and if we are to learn to value the inherent intelligences of our own bodies, well then, we must be taught about them. Where does one start on a matter as complex as the body? That's what my mind is thinking now, just to share that with you. I'll be honest, I have indeed wondered where all of this is coming from, but the answer is easy; I lived it, learned it and now it's time to try and teach it. But by crikey, my system is enjoying its own little fear bursts as I attempt to expand into the unknown—i.e. believing in myself, that's still a challenging concept for my mind to adhere to, even now as I sit typing this, my first book for adults. However, it is the very awareness of this fear arising in my body and mind that allows me to move past it.

Fear is uncomfortable, that's why we avoid feeling it. But what is the feeling of fear actually? How does it manifest in the body? Well, to me it's a swirl of sensation, sometimes it might begin in my gut, a weight, an invisible heaviness without a known origin, it simply exists and travels up into my chest where it sits as a restrictive flutter, signalling for me to stop whatever is happening. And then there're the deeper fears, the ones I touch on when I really push at my boundaries, ones like love, physical intimacy or honest vulnerability. Well, when I touch on these energetic wounds of the past Little Miss Crazy likes to come out to dance, at least that's what others may see. What I actually experience may be termed as temporary depressions, anxiety, or trauma triggering; I too may experience physical and debilitating pain in my sternum and heart centre, and silent screams have even escaped me.

It's fair to say that my life experiences have weighed heavy on the scale in the way of trauma and the scars run deep, but my passion is finding said scars, poking at them a little until they rip open and bleed all over the place. Then I sit and look at what that wound was made up of, what memories, thoughts, feelings and projections erupted within me as they were being triggered up to the surface, before processing and releasing whatever it was that belonged to the past. I don't know where these things live, I just know they exist inside of me and that they don't belong in there.

The wounds of my past have interfered with my present and this has been my only torture in life. I did not choose the experiences that I lived, yet they kept me caged for half a lifetime. The battle I fought for freedom inside of myself was one with no witness, it is a battle I fought and won alone, but it is one to let go of now. My body doesn't even want that story anymore either, it likes to let go and forget these days, I trained it to do so. Or rather, I allowed it to do what it was designed to, I just had to clear out the garbage that was in there clogging up the system, I had to slaughter that elephant in the room. It seems logical to assert that back when I lived certain experiences, I hadn't yet learned to allow the body to feel, process and release things as they happened, so these experiences became trapped within my body and mind. No one taught me my body could do that, but apparently it can.

CHAPTER 5

The Flow of Things...

You see, when I live an experience, I am no longer a big ball of living reaction, which, I'm afraid, is all most of us are at any given time. Don't get me wrong, my humanness comes out to play whether I like it or not, but I experience things in a less passive manner these days. As I live an experience, I simultaneously observe both the external trigger and the internal reactions, then turn to consider the connection between the two and observe any patterns or cycles that emerge in my own behaviour.

Let me provide an example: for a lot of my teenage years I struggled with weight gain, it was a side effect of heavy medical steroid prescriptions I received for a chronic illness. To live your teens carrying unwelcome and unearned weight is a devastation, especially when combined with the perceptions and cruelty of others. We all know the names people use to cause pain in the other and I heard these words on and off for a decade as I struggled with my health, at no fault of my own. When I lived in Southeast Asia, around the time I started fighting that internal battle I mentioned, an old friend of mine came to visit, Little Miss Over-Eater; in other words, I got a bit fat, and this time it really was of my own doing.

Living this experience revealed a lot of things that lived inside of me, as social norms meant locals were perfectly permitted to comment on the changes in my body and tell me that I was indeed fat and looked better before. These words hurt, but the difference was that I couldn't take them personally as they were spoken without malice or cruelty of intent. I promise you, the observations of my fatness were always kindly delivered and seemed to behold the same innocence found in the verbal outbursts of a child. They helped me forgive others, they helped me heal when I realized that the pain I felt inside at hearing these words had nothing to do with those individuals. It had to do with that word being used in my childhood home, it had to do with the time a boy called me fat in front of friends and shamed me publicly for a painful struggle I lived with daily, it had to do with those years of looking in the mirror and hating myself, wishing for change, but it never really feeling achievable.

*I had a massive mental block on believing
that I could look and feel beautiful.*

I never believed it was possible to feel anything but ugly and loathe myself, if I'm honest, I didn't even know that was what I felt until I started feeling something different. Even during those periods in life when I was physically fit and slender, my mind still believed the other stuff and I never got to see and appreciate the reality of myself, even when that reality was something quite lovely. It was one of the most wonderful and saddening days when I realized my own beauty, when I got to look in the mirror at my own face and see what it had really looked like for all of these years. It was a miracle to me, but one not understood by anyone I spoke to, yet I was free in some new way, free to like myself. As I looked at my petite, soft and unconditioned body, I started to enjoy the way my butt wobbled and the new softness found in my maturing breasts. I started to believe the people who, for all of these years, told me I had beautiful blue eyes. I started to see myself a little more clearly, and this was after the first wrinkle started showing on my forehead.

Another story that popped into my head was, 'No matter what I do, I'll never be fit and healthy. It's just not possible for me.' This was of course not true, I'd been fit and healthy and proved this internal voice wrong many a time, but it was stubborn as heck, which was understandable as it was a belief constantly reinforced during adolescence and early adulthood as a result of those steroid treatments. These stories about myself and my body I no longer believe, and it has been such a relief to my system releasing these experiences and throwing them in the garbage where they belong. Liberation from my own mind is the only liberation I seek, mostly because my ancestors battled for the many other kinds of freedoms I am blessed with. A battle still being fought so that I might live the life that I do is that of the feminist.

I watched a movie the other day with Keira Knightly in the lead, *Collette*, about a female ghost writer whose talent was claimed by her husband. This happened for two reasons: the husband thought he had a right to own her voice; and the world held more value over a man's voice than a woman's. It was a double-edged sword at her throat. Yet here I sit in a house owned solely by a woman, writing to my heart's content and holding no fear in my heart that because I am a female my voice will be rejected by the world. However, that's not quite true, is it? In many places around the world women still live to fill the form of man's desire, be that by cooking, cleaning, mothering, or even becoming their preferred punching bag. In the woman's fight for equality, she fought to be afforded the same opportunities as man, to prove she could do things his way, to prove she was no lesser species, it was necessary in order to carve a path in this man's world.

But that path has been carved and I am now here following a way that others trudged before me, I am here knowing that I am allowed to sit and write because other women ignored the voice in their head that told them they couldn't. Other women ignored the stories the world told them and liberated a lineage from oppressive mind sets that were resulting in limited lives being lived. The same can be said of any other warriors of light who walk a path that shines on the collective illusions of humankind's mind, be those stories of racism, homophobia or any other pain-causing prejudice. It is only ever fear of the unknown that keeps us in judgement and conflict, when we think we know something the other person doesn't. But we really need to start looking at what we think we know and where it came from if we are to harmonize a world tipping beyond imbalance.

Anytime you judge someone else, do the right thing, look at yourself first. I remember the first time the nonsense of my own mind came to my attention, I was walking along the beach in Bali at twenty-five years old and there was a young man wearing matching shorts, shoes, bag and hat, and my nasty little mind said, 'What a geek.' I was horrified by my own thought, truly. What had this possibly delightful soul ever done to deserve such a thought thrown his way? I hated that the thought was even there and quickly changed the story to celebrate his bold choice to be an individual. You see, that thought, 'Geek,' well that's probably an extension of the thought that prevented me from dressing like Avril Lavigne when I was fifteen and kept me sticking to more conservative choices of attire.

The funny thing is, I was already a geek, oh the shame of being smart, I loved every minute of school and time spent in learning. The other learners, they were mostly a hinderance to the internal thirst for knowledge that I had from a young age and, for the most part, annoyed me senseless. The girls labelled as cool who brought alcohol to school in Fanta bottles and let off fire extinguishers in the corridors all ended up living the same lives as one another, they all lived a similar collective experience of predictable repetition. Cool never drew me in though, I only ever saw something I'd rather not be. How ridiculous it is that humans are so intimidated by one another's beautiful gifts and qualities that we make them hide beneath shame and retreat from expressing their true self out into the world? People scared of their own stupidity and mundane existence feed on denying others the right to be different, for if *they* are wrong then their whole world will crumble as it loses meaning and sense.

Be brave people, be bold enough to discover who you are, ignore the stories of old and let's make some new ones. If stories are what we learn, I have come to wonder whether we can learn what it is to truly love one another. I don't know that there are many stories of love in the world, not really, perhaps this is why people cling with such desperate blind faith to religion, because these stories are so full of the unconditional love that we all crave yet haven't learned to give or receive for ourselves. We look to the movies and books to show us what love is, but they do not reveal love, they only present an image of need and want, and there's a big difference. Yet books of faith, they point the way to something, that's what they're there to do, show you what's not true about yourself.

> *Every experience lived presents a mirror*
> *in which to see yourself, every single one.*

It is the scariest thing to do, look in the mirror of reality and see yourself and your life, mostly because we don't like what we see and why would we? Can you think back to the last time that not a problem existed in your world, the last time you were simply and utterly happy to be alive for an extended period of time? I think for most of us it may well be childhood that pops up as the destination of any true answer one might come to. Children don't have problems unless we tell them they exist; problems aren't real until we're programmed to believe they are. What is a problem but a denial of reality as it stands? A problem is something we fix, but what does fix mean? It means to alter a reality we are dissatisfied with. Why do we feel the need to do this? Why, as humans, do we have this incessant need for more, faster, bigger, stronger, better?

'Man' is the word that just popped in my mind, is it because man made this world and it reflects his characteristic survival mentality? Is it because his need to protect and present symbolic strength developed into patterns of greed and oppression? I really do think that the voice of the feminine is here to balance the planet in some way, but I think for some of us ladies, the fight is over, we get to live free now. Wow, I just cried and continue to do so as I feel the power of these words...

I am a free woman.

I've never felt it before, this feeling I'm experiencing as I type these words. I am so grateful to those women who made this life possible for me, the men too, who were brave enough to allow their minds to morph and grow as reality presented different truths to the ones they were born to. Change is always brave and as I sit here, I start to suddenly feel so brave myself, I have endured and I have survived one heck of a life, but it is one I am no longer a victim of.

You know, I think I'm learning what it means to be a free woman, to be a woman free of the stories we've been woven in for millennia. The world made space for a new kind of woman to emerge, a woman more connected to the nature of herself and willing to express this out loud, even as it continues to be labelled as sensitive, delicate, overreactive, illogical or unreasonable. Yet I am none of these things. Man's world taught me logic and reason, but I think these were only parts of the puzzle. I am a creature made up of emotion and man is too, it's just that after thousands of years battling to survive, defend and kill, of course his emotional body became somewhat numb to the full spectrum of lived emotion.

However, woman, having a physique built for breeding, not fighting, did not have to shut down her emotional body, but man did that for her anyway, just to a lesser extent. You see, that same fear that breeds racism, that was the same fear that made man squash the emotional and intuitive voice of woman. Fear of the other. Fear of the unknown. Fear of feeling. It wasn't man's fault, the experiences that he lived were too unbearable to feel, and I imagine, as the tenderness of a woman touched on his internal wounds they threatened to open. And not knowing how to identify, manage or deal with the experience, they went on to live a denial of self and avoidance of reality. Feeling connects feeling, there is no disconnect between two people as an energetic exchange is lived, this is just physics and chemistry.

CHAPTER 6

Connection

All is connected. All is one. The invisible transparent space between two humans is no empty vacuum, there lies a complex series of energetic happenings that we quantify into meaning by use of words such as energy, vibration, frequency, chemical reaction, matter. You know what, this all makes sense to me, I can picture it all happening in and around me. That's what I do, visualize lived experiences as energetic happenings, I see the spoken word delivered as a flow of sound and feel the impact on my physical body. I receive the vibration of this occurrence and observe the consequent reactions ripple through my being and am fascinated by the way they always result in something arising internally. We react all of the time as a result of our connectedness with the external environment, just as a plant reacts to sunlight or a gazelle reacts to its predator.

> *Something in the external environment*
> *happens and our 'system-of-self' responds,*
> *in whatever way it's been programmed to.*

Let's take love for instance, or I'd rather use the word *intimacy*, for love is too often a misinterpreted need being met, an act attempting to fill a lack left over from childhood. Let's look at various possible reactions to intimacy; my reaction, for example, was a long-standing nothing, if I was touched on the shoulder by a handsome man or kissed even, I would have zero reaction, why? I was frozen inside. I had lived an ongoing series of traumatic experiences for such a prolonged length of time that it resulted in my fight-or-flight system getting jammed into frozen mode, possibly because it was in overdrive constantly and it is unbearable to live, physiologically, within a constant state of terror.

However, the way my mind coped with it all was to make up some wonderful stories that made it all bearable. All we must do to see the mind's various survival mechanisms is to look at Stockholm Syndrome, when captives are suggested to develop a survival-based affection for their captors. In other words, they align with a mindset that is more certain to ensure their survival, both internally and externally, a submission to a hopefully temporary reality of sorts. Anyway, I think maybe because I lived very few reactions, at least not many that I ever let another person see, I became fascinated by the reactions presented by others.

Here's an interesting example: during my mid-teen years my friends and I would frequent, *The Pool Hall*. It gave us something to do instead of walk around aimlessly or be confined to a parental home, and more importantly at fifteen/sixteen years old, it was a place that served underaged drinkers. My group of friends was boy heavy, most of us knowing one another from Army Cadets. This was a young person's social club of sorts that helped challenge me to come out of my shy little shell and find out a little more about who I was, for I didn't live in a world that helped me do that, I don't know how many of us really do. Because of my fear of intimacy, I became very good at being friends with boys, I wanted nothing from them and as soon as they realized that they weren't getting in my knickers anytime soon, they wanted nothing more than friendship from me either.

Let's talk about the other girls for a moment, the ones that giggled when a boy poked at their ribs, those who bent over a table as guys 'helped them learn' how to shoot pool. I'll be honest, this behaviour confused me and I found little respect for it. I found the girls' need for that kind of attention diminishing of her actual worth, and I found the boys' interest in it transparent as their sexed-up little minds went on the hunt. The drama of the teenage love triangles, or pentagons as it was at times with our extended group of friends, well, it was not something I involved myself in. I simply watched it all go down, and oh my, did it go down. No one had taught these girls self-respect, but you know what, no one had taught me either, my grace was that I was simply too petrified for anyone to come near me. I was the girl the lads didn't lay, I was the one the lads talked to and confided in, a rare female that lived without reacting to them, I suppose. It wasn't by any means healthy, my way of being, but it does mean that I've lived with the privilege of becoming rather close to many males over the years.

I have learned so very much about men and I think my nearest and dearest would allow me to say that their minds really do revolve around sex a lot of the time. Just like a dog in heat, when the physiological moment strikes as a result of the appropriate external stimuli, enter, the attractive lady, it's pretty much game on. All men find their own way of playing the game because they are just as complex as women, they can be shy, insecure, jealous, fearful of intimacy, abandonment and rejection, and this all informs their own mating patterns and rituals. Like a delicate dance, two suitors ask and answer questions, gauging the playing field to see if the responses of the other leave them with a pleasurable or less pleasurable resulting feeling and experience.

What determines whether an experience is pleasurable or less so? Simply put, it all stems from how you react to it.

Let's say you're on a date and the other person tells a story about their dad who was an alcoholic, one whom they exorcised from their life because they believed he was just a selfish man. Yet you also have an alcoholic father, one whom you have maintained a profound and great compassion for as you watched him powerlessly slip into the grips of addiction, a debilitating and life-threatening mental health disease. Side note: addiction is science guys—get to grips with it and change the story, I beg of you, too many lives to count depend on it.

No addict is selfish. No addict is cruel, weak, or doing it on purpose. They are sick in a different way, a way not fully understood or recognized by the world. They need help. They don't often know or recognize it, but they do. They need you to be the adult and LOVE THEM PROPERLY, stop fearing them not loving you back because you must make tough choices, stop being selfish. Love them first and embody consistent honesty, this is the best form of love for an addict, never let them forget their true reality, for that's what they are always trying to escape, don't let them, the longer you let them escape, the harder they are to find down the line.

Well now, let's get back to that date, can you see how these two powerful stories lived hold the power to create an immediate conflict? Two internal belief systems relating to two core figures in two separate threads of life, how can there not be conflict? If they are good at self-regulating, meaning they can feel their feelings internally without blurting out every reaction that pops into their mind, they may make it through the date and leave it at that. Another positive outcome might be that the compassionate mind-set carefully counters with gentle examples of why they still love and support their father and help the other begin a journey of letting go as they understand their own anger and resentment in a new way, when they learn to accept responsibility for their own pain. As a contrast, perhaps the person with firm and distant boundaries lives this way with a necessity for survival and teaches the supposed compassionate person that they are self-sacrificing and identifies their kindness as another form of enabling.

All interactions have many outcomes, dependent on the interplay of a lived sequence of shared happenings beyond our control, yet not beyond our awareness. The reason every lived experience is beyond our control is because it always involves *The Other*. I don't know how to describe

The Other in this moment because I have suddenly come to contemplate whether it could embody any lived experience shared with external energy sources and stimuli. The world is complex, and I like to try and make it a little simpler, so from now on *The Other* can refer to all external happenings. When you consider yourself as you sit and watch the T.V, you are living reactions all of the time, fear at the latest news, sadness at a death in a movie, adrenaline in reaction to a high-speed car chase in a Jason Bourne movie. The Other is always triggering you, always.

> *Yet how can we distinguish 'The Self' from 'The Other',*
> *when we are The Other, to other people's Self?*

Do you see the problem with thought and its own limitations? When exploring new concepts that can only be imagined, Einstein employed a tool called *thought experiments,* whereby he visualized a happening beyond physical recognition, all while ensuring it was well-informed by logical and reasoned arguments. That's what we're doing here today, getting used to thinking of lived experiences as *thought experiments.* Can you imagine waves of sound rippling towards you and contacting your being as The Other projects various words and vibrations outward, and consider the varying physical and mental reactions that might present within you as a result? Everybody reacts differently to different words spoken in their direction or to a different song being played. Our likes and dislikes can become one of our greatest tells, but how many of us think beyond this lived reaction and learn to read into ourselves?

CHAPTER 7

80% Water, Really?

So, remember that sculptor of stone I mentioned, Silvio? Well, he once demonstrated to me the live impact of sound upon water when he placed a small saucer of H2O onto one of the three great slabs of stone that made up this giant xylophone-like musical instrument, and then shined a red light onto the reflective surface. As he created long oval-like shapes and waves of infinity with his beater, dragging it gently across the sculpted rocks, my ears heard a new sound and my eyes watched the water dance. A kaleidoscope of light rippled across the surface as I watched an invisible vibration of sound impact this water and result in a visual spectacle. Something pricked inside of me, this same magic I saw twinkling before my eyes must happen to my physical body when it is met with vibrations of various kinds. I started recognizing how my body moved of its own accord when it was met with music, how it flowed and danced in different ways according to the style of song being played.

I slowly started realizing that my body knew exactly what it was meant to do, I simply had to let it.

That's half the problem in life you see, we don't realize our own innate intelligences, the very ones we're born with. I think we might even fear them and therefore smother our natural way of being with stories about what we should be, rather than learn to accept what we are. And what are we but a unique species of animal? The observable impact of music is not only evidenced in dancing humans. Elephants have been disposed to enjoying the piano, appearing to even find it soothing and healing, whilst other animals and even plants have been observed to react positively to the right vibrational stimulus. In other words, every living thing seems to respond in variety when presented with vibrations of sound delivered from different sources.

Our intelligent human body is so clever that it can discern which sounds are good for us and help to identify those that are perhaps less healthy. The human gauge for this is known as the spectrum of human emotion; however, I would argue that it's set a little off kilter. In this moment I remember back to my first interactions with horror movies, the likes of

Nightmare on Elm Street and *Texas Chainsaw Massacre*, I was about fifteen years old when I started watching these. I remember enjoying the sensation of fear, which can perhaps be likened to the sensation of aliveness. Fear is what we meet when we say hello to a new and unknown experience and horror movies stimulate the same physiological adrenaline rush as a first-time bungy jump or when one rides a wave on the Pacific Ocean. But there is one big difference: one is a lived experience, the other is the illusion of a lived experience.

When a person watches a movie, they become a passive receiver of a designed reality, they absorb sound and projections of light that form meaning within the mind, the received images and sounds are then responded to in various ways. I've only ever met one man who truly abstains from watching T.V. But do you know what my friend, Bill, does in the meantime? He lives life. He rides horses, climbs trees, expands his culinary skills, writes, paints, plays music, and all whilst being an active and involved husband and father. We all have so many excuses in the way of truly living, but Bill, I don't know that I've ever heard him create an imaginary problem, perhaps because he hasn't absorbed them from the main source of collective mind sets, the media and popular culture.

I asked the question a couple of months ago, do teenagers

FAITH

drink and have promiscuous sex because it's 'normal,' and then 'normal' is what's presented on T.V? Or has all the sexually driven T.V. narrative massively influenced how young people deliver themselves to the world? Community is dead and role models are few and far between, where are young minds to look for examples of a life lived well and happily? A little over a year ago I was sitting in the back of a 4x4 cruising through the varying terrain of the La Guajira Desert, Colombia, when something hit me - we never stop being toddlers, we never stop looking to the external world for cues on how to act or what to say and think. Consider this for a moment, every child born to the earth learns to be human by way of observation and imitation. And do you know what I saw these Colombian children doing, these tiny humans aged between two and ten? I saw them playing at begging, presenting a sad foreboding of their lives-to-be.

After years of travel, the witnessing of extreme poverty was nothing new to me. But the doors of common travel have only been open for a decade or so in Colombia, thus, the desert is newly explored terrain and no fantastical story has yet been woven to entice tourists into a well-delivered, false presentation of reality. For the modern-day traveller, making it to the most northern tip of South America is a fresh feat, one that makes visible the early devastations of the tourism industry. What was once a way of life has become poverty and suffering, as people once harmonized with their land are forced to pay for the basic needs that they once met for themselves. They are forced to stand at the side of the road and accept scraps from passing cars, said scraps are disguised as a tourist toll payment, but all they receive is 250ml of water or, not *and*, *or*, three Mini Oreo cookies.

The devastation ran deep, but what made matters worse was that as these children ran with ropes across the car, imitating the stop posts of their parents, the four tourists accompanying me found it amusing. One of the saddest things I'd ever seen was making these people laugh, which is what tipped me over the edge and left me crying silent tears as I looked out of the window and watched two men riding a single bicycle through winds that cut like sandpaper.

Reality is in the eye of the beholder.
Please do start asking what story your mind is telling.

When you walk past a homeless person do you see a nuisance? Do you make excuses in your mind to help release the shame of not shouting him a few bucks? Or do you see a whole human living a less than fortunate experience? Let's remember the three things that make us a lucky human: food, water and shelter. A homeless person lacks one of life's basic needs and in doing so misses out on any sense of safety or feeling of security, two essentialities of a healthy life.

You know, I often find it interesting how the world perfectly permits pessimistic mind sets. It allows false excuses to be formed and the truth to be hidden beneath the blankets of our own shame and insecurity. A homeless person has close to nothing, yet we wager in our heads as to their actual level of suffering and wonder whether they are simply '...one of those professional beggars.' Professional or not, on the street is not how I'd prefer to spend my limited days on this planet spinning in space.

Whatever the reasons you have for judging, shaming or ridiculing someone in a less fortunate circumstance than you, well, throw those reasons away. There are never any valid reasons for this, there is only ever a single person smothering their own discomfort at an external stimulus with thoughts that make it all a little more comfortable. We like to tell stories about reality that make it more digestible, we like to think that the £3 a month we give to Oxfam really does help those dying babies in Africa we've seen on the T.V. since before we could talk.

We like to dismiss the world's problems because we weren't the ones who made them, that, or we simply feel overwhelmed by the number of problems there are to solve and so shrivel into our shell of complete and utter powerlessness. But I tell you this, there are no problems, not really, something is only ever a problem if you let your mind believe it is. I could identify Gaza as a problem of the world, but it's not, it's a problem for the people of Gaza. I do not say this without compassion, of course I would wish something different for all people living in a state of perpetual suffering. What I mean to say is, the wars of other places are not my problem, heck, the affairs of my neighbour are not even my problem. I have come to learn, after some hard knocks from life, that it is not within my power to change the world, the only thing I might ever accomplish in changing is myself, and the same goes for the rest of you.

My responsibility is me, no one else, at least until I perhaps become a mother, and until that day the greatest feat I might accomplish is to become the lightest and most joyful version of myself. To work on oneself is a challenge like no other, to face the truth of oneself is the bravest of work. To admit to your own dysfunction and distaste of your actual reality requires one to drop any sense of denial and face the facts of their life and themselves. This is what one might call a mid-life crisis, that time in a person's life when everything becomes meaningless and they realize that they bought into the false tale of happiness they were spoon fed since birth.

Many of us reach the end of the rainbow and realize there is no pot of gold, only more rainbow...

FAITH

Life doesn't end until death, but we all seem to be rushing towards an early grave, giving up on life from the onset of adulthood and surrendering to this simply being the way of things. I never believed it, not for one second, something inside of me always let me know that this life I was blessed with was here to be *lived*. For a long time, I debated within myself what it meant to live my life fully and I was desperate for a definition of both purpose and meaning. Life felt devoid of something, empty, like wherever I went I couldn't find what I was looking for.

I began adulthood by dedicating myself to the teaching profession, hoping to change the world one tiny, adorable mind at a time, but was met with the oppressive and controlling nature of education systems. I tried charity work and delivered myself to a remote orphanage in the western mountains of Bali, only to find my own powerlessness to save any single child devastatingly crippling. I contemplated working for a mainstream charity, but found that my skillset and experience were not something to be valued and was instructed at every turn to 'start from the bottom up.' I had too much to offer to become an underpaid paper pusher. No offense to paper pushers, I rather enjoyed pushing paper at seventeen years old, I'd simply moved beyond it.

I stayed in month-long yoga retreats, including the seeing

through of a particularly gruelling Ayurvedic full-body detox in India, which pretty much involved the engagement of every orifice present on my body at some point or another, as well as more nudity amongst strangers than I ever expected to experience in a lifetime. I spent time throwing myself into the uncomfortable and scary, tentatively testing my own limitations and learning to move beyond them. The only blocks that ever existed were in my mind, and I started to notice that there were particular thoughts and feelings arising as I met new experiences. Let's take dance as an example; I lived my life as a closet dancer, if you were a fly on my teenage bedroom wall then you'd have enjoyed a daily show. But somewhere along the way that stopped, just as it does for so many of us, and adulthood seemed to swallow me whole.

A few years ago, I was walking along the coastline of Pfeiffer State Park, California, when I had the happy coincidence of meeting Rob, a guy in a wheelchair making videos about something curious. I paused, so as not to interrupt filming, and then enquired as to what he was up to. Rob explained that at sixteen years old he broke his neck and has been tetraplegic ever since, but that he found his way to a joyful existence and so spends time making videos for those who meet a similar fate. It is his hope that he might provide comfort and inspiration to others who are met with such a dramatic life-changing circumstance.

It was one of the more profound meetings of my life, on this cliff edge facing the Pacific Ocean. Accompanying Rob were two others, Shane and Tarn, the start-up film crew and friends of the man in question. I was invited to couch surf that night, which was an invitation I happily accepted, and was later blessed with my poetry being turned into song. Shane recorded a local singer, full of soul, perform the poem as she lived her own journey of self-expansion. An excitement lingers as I sit, yet to listen to the final bass track that Shane and Tarn created, whatever happened that night remaining unheard by my ears. It was a beautiful meet and it only seems appropriate to share the poem, *I Am Love*, here. Please enjoy:

I am not the body,
Decaying, growing old.
I am not persona,
Garbed and masked as told.

I am not the mind,
Babbling incessantly within.
I am not emotion,
To let go is to begin.

I am neither hate nor anger,
Perpetuated from outside.
I am not the fear,
In me it shall not reside.

I am not false happiness,
Constructed by a material world.
I am not the false being,
Truth shall one day be unfurled.

Yet, I am not the lost soul,
Thirsting for an answer.
Nor am I the disciple,
For I do not have a master.

I am not what is seen or heard,
Lie and illusion are told by sense.
But born amidst awareness is truth,
A peace, a great presence.

I am Love.
I am Love.
I am Love.

It was the sharing of magic found in those moments that I treasure, as well as the feeling I had toward being seen and heard for who I was, even more, feeling valued for being her. It was a new experience and something difficult to walk away from after only twenty-four hours, but I felt lighter and left with more faith and trust in what was to come. I have quoted Rob many a time since that day, you see, the main questions he asks people are, 'What's fun for you? What do you enjoy?' My immediate answer back then was, 'Dancing,' and he saw my whole self light up at the thought of it alone. I then went on to note that I also loved joyful jam sessions, painting with the skill set of a six-year-old, as well as writing, for it was with these people that I first had the courage to call myself a writer.

I was an artist my entire life and I never knew it. This devastated me. I thought my life was over the day I realized I had never really known who I was, but lucky me, little did I know the fun of it all had only just begun...

CHAPTER 8

Time Ticks On, Always and Forever

It has been two years between calling myself a writer and sitting down to commit to writing. What stood in the way? Nothing but a whole load of self-doubt and other junk that wasn't real. I spent years waiting for somebody to give me permission to speak my voice, for someone to tell me that what I wanted to say was worth listening to. And really, that's still a lie, what I was waiting for was for my own self-belief to propel me into action. The same self-doubt that stands between you and a cartwheel is the very same doubt that keeps you in denial of yourself and what you really truly want. And deep down we all yearn for the same thing, to know, be and love ourselves; yet we look to the external world for this key to our freedom, we wait for the world to love us and guide us home, but it never does. That, we can only ever do for ourselves.

'What do you do when you know what you like?' I asked Rob on our first and only evening together. His response came with a knowing and happy smile, 'Just choose to do it more often.' Simple. Profound. Concise. The answer we're all looking for? We really do waste so much of our precious time, the only truly limited commodity we have, doing plenty of things we don't like. We are all on our way out from the moment we take our first breath, that's just a fact. Why not really sit with that actuality for a moment... One day you will be dead, you will cease to exist. One day, even the memory of you will be gone, as you fade into time and dust. And the thing that scares people senseless, so much so that they cease to live in the first place, is the reality of that last breath potentially being tomorrow. So what if it is? It is only a person who lives with regret that dies with regret. So, I say live fully and regret nothing.

What is regret but a memory of a moment
when we let fear get the better of us?
When our hearts told us to act,
but we let that pull of the safe and familiar
call us back into our comfort zones?

Fear keeps us frozen in time and space, living a life of perpetual cyclic repeat. Fear is something we are born free of and come to learn and inherit from the lives of those who lived before us. The fear of not enough is what presents and manifests in a hoarder, it is the same thing that keeps a shopaholic spending crippling amounts of money, just as it is the primal cause and root of any patterns of addiction. That same life-threatening fear felt by a human experiencing starvation is the very same fear that keeps an alcoholic trapped in their own cage of pain and suffering—*the fear of not enough*, because ultimately, we are programmed with the inherent belief that 'not enough' leads to certain death.

This is what an addict is fighting, their own body, mind and system telling them that their very survival is dependent on that next fix, that next illusion of a necessary need being met. It's built into the brain, it's predictable in nature and is a disease that presents symptoms as the visibly lived consequences of long-term addiction. For those not familiar with the symptoms of addiction, they run as follows: destroy your life, body and mind, watch powerlessly as your loved ones try to save you, break your own heart every time you break theirs. Hidden is the reality of an addict, hidden beneath their pain, trauma and shame. It is the most selfish thing to blame an addict for anything, this is the truth. I speak these words for my sister, I speak these words for every person living with addiction whose life is limited by this embedded fear of not enough.

Addictions fuel this world and its greed and it is something very real that plagues us as a species, and it's something very scarily starting at a younger and younger age. Technology, a juggernaut of change, a force propelling the evolution of our own species beyond any it may have lived before, is a worrying source of addictive patterns. With any new discovery comes change, at first these discoveries were material, little pockets of starlight energy trapped within the earth waiting to be discovered and manipulated by humans. Here, I'm referring to those periods of time which have been labelled with their own source of change, The Stone Age, The Iron Age, The Industrial Revolution and Age of Enlightenment. Now change manifests *internally*, as the way we function and fundamentally connect becomes ever further removed from our natural functioning state.

As aforementioned, we are living in the midst of The Technological Revolution. There are small periods in history labelled as such, but I would argue that they were evidently the beginning of a revolution that we are still living today, and possibly one with no end. The discoveries made today not only enrich and expand one's life, they also seem to observably contract a person's existence and replace human connection with the illusion of it. Technology serves a grand many purposes in this world and I am not a hater of it. I love the easy access to music and the fact that I no longer have to sit by a radio with my finger over the pause button if I want to record a song on tape and play it on repeat. Better yet, I don't even have to rewind to replay, I just click a little button. Technology rocks, let's face it, I just feel like we need to get a bit better at defining where it belongs in life and establishing healthy informed boundaries around it, to protect ourselves and our lives from a potentially devastating epidemic of new addictive patterns.

Just look at 'gamers,' none of whom I know, but who supposedly look at a T.V. screen for hours on end and are drawn into an imaginary world whereby they live some half-real version of reality. This has become so socially acceptable that a whole industry is built around this addiction. Watching television daily is no different, nor gambling, overeating or anything else in excess that throws your life off balance somehow. We are often too quick to judge without taking an honest look at ourselves, but, 'Let he without sin cast the first stone,' and all that.

I was pondering the seven deadly sins not so long ago, and as far as I can tell, all each sin resembles is an aspect of self that, when left in dominant unchecked states, leaves an unhealthy imprint on your life. Let's look at some powerful polarities set to contrast the good against the bad of the world: light vs. dark, pride vs. humility, gluttony vs. prudence, lust vs. love, greed vs. pleasing, anger vs. meekness. The fact is, swing too far in any direction and you are met with an imbalance that can manifest in infinite unhealthy ways. There is far too much judgement surrounding our own conceptualization of humanness, we are our own harshest critics and are never taught that these colourful aspects of self are okay, they are normal in fact. For I believe that it is when we stop ignoring these somewhat unsavoury parts of ourselves that they lessen in power and begin to diminish.

The only way is *through,* there is no way of avoiding some of the harsher truths about oneself if a person wishes for any sort of change or improvement to happen in life. No one is going to give you the answer, no one is going to sell you a miracle and change your life for you, only you can do this. So, if you are sitting there now dissatisfied with something about your existence, I'm here to tell you that life doesn't have to be this way, things can be different, they can be okay, if you realize they already are. We hear that a lot, don't we? *Everything is going to be okay.* Well my experience says otherwise, rare are the moments in my world when anything happening in the external could be deemed as 'okay,' by collective standards. But that's only if I let my mind accept that there is a problem with how reality presents itself to me.

It was some months ago now, but I was headed for bed in my little bungalow sat atop an opposing jungle valley view, when I decided to check in with family in England. It was a conversation during which I learned that my sister, whose addiction had led to her injecting heroine, had not been seen for a week and that she was officially off the radar. As I hung up the phone, I watched my own mind turn to despair, I saw an image form of my sister stretching a makeshift tourniquet around her upper arm before injecting and releasing an induced high into her system. I quickly pressed pause on this thought as I realized that the only reference I had for it was Hollywood movies, and I comforted myself with the fact that she could be sitting in a café eating lunch, or even better, sleeping and letting her body and mind rest. You see, I love my sister, she is one of my favourite humans, and it has been one of the greatest devastations to stand by and watch a person I grew up with slowly become a ghost of their former self.

The real heart-breaking moments are when they come back to you for a flash, when you see that they are still in there, still fighting their own battle somehow, and you wish you could just help them win. My sister has fought long and hard for her health and sanity, yet society does not recognize her needs and therefore they go unmet. I am happy to say that recovery seems to be in motion, but it is a tentative process and one I have absolutely no influence over. I do believe it is by learning to love my sister and let go of any need for her to heal for my sake that I have learned what it truly means to love another. I know my sis, I know her heart, the kind woman beneath the trauma, and it is that person whom I still see today. I no longer patronize my sister with words such as lost, choice, or readiness. These words cannot be used where addiction is concerned, there is no being ready for treatment and recovery, there is only ever the doing of the thing.

There is never a moment when you are ready to fight for your life, I think for most it might happen by accident, but once the intention is set, once one step is taken on the path, every subsequent step becomes a little easier. I think for many the thing that lies between active addiction and active recovery is a little self-forgiveness and self-love. Self-love is a term thrown around a lot these days, it has become another slogan, another hook people use to sell you a false answer that supposedly solves the problem of your own dissatisfaction and unhappiness. Quite often, the people who create these solutions are the same people to have created the illusion of the problem in the first place.

I lived my whole young life being told there was something wrong with my body and the way it looked. It was a normal thing to go to the shop and buy a magazine as a teenager, but now that I look back, I am horrified by the images that were presented to me. Strikingly beautiful women celebrated when they were groomed to perfection, yet shamed and ridiculed for the human moments they lived, be it eating a slice of cake, sporting a few spots of cellulite at the beach or god forbid, blinking at the same time the photo was being taken. All I saw was a world that hated the natural body of the woman and which inspired an image of unobtainable beauty. To my increasing incredulity, I've just had a flashback of both men and women being given marks out of ten for certain superficial characteristics. I was born to a world that didn't like or value who I was, and I can't tell you how much pain this has caused me in life.

I think back now to an early meeting with one of my best young friends, Kala, she was twelve years old at the time and exploring what it meant as her body started to change. Beautiful as she is, she was drawn to modelling, a brutal environment for a young body and mind unless they enter it with a certain level of self-awareness and self-esteem. As she scrolled the internet for images of the female form, she started to compare herself and discuss how she could modify her young developing body. My inner alarm bells rang, I saw the same traps waiting for her, the same journey of self-loathing fuelled by a comparison with this well-presented illusion of perfection. I immediately directed her towards reality, and we watched videos of airbrushing, observing how they sculpt and shape the body digitally, alter the tone of a model's skin and change the features of the face.

> *The advertising industry quite literally creates imaginary people based on what lines and shapes are pleasing to the eye.*

On top of this, we talked about how supermodels have been known to eat cotton wool soaked in orange juice to sustain energy and quench starvation pangs before walking on the catwalk, and ultimately burst the bubble of any of this being real or something to aspire to. Knowledge is power. In this case, knowledge had the power to partially free a young developing mind and body from the cruelly presented lies about how she should look. The world doesn't tell you how perfect you already are, it doesn't teach you to celebrate the wonder of your own physiology and tune into what it's actually asking for, sustainable nourishment. All it does is take advantage of your vulnerable, unknowing and defenceless inner world by using your very nature to direct and manipulate your almost absolute existence. For it wasn't too many years ago that the abuse of subliminal messaging was banned in cinema theatres when money makers manipulated the minds of their customers and programmed them to buy more food and drink.

The use and abuse of knowledge is chronic, and it is a new battle that humankind is facing, a battle of the mind. Our once natural surroundings have shifted over the last half-century into something beyond recognition, with talking screens, moving pictures and instant cross-global communication. It is a wonder as to what our species will shortly become if we do not equip our minds with defence mechanisms against an ever intrusive and brain-washing world. Moreover, it is the vulnerable minds of the young that we must protect from these unknown environmental influences and educate ourselves, as well as them, on how to survive the daily sensory onslaught of stuff and nonsense.

CHAPTER 9

Protecting Our Young

It is our responsibility as adults to inform our interactions and practices with children. Personally, I think it is something that should be taught at school, since predictively a very many students will go on to procreate. Just as I consider first aid to be a welcome life skill for all, so too do I believe that tiny humans need to be taught how to communicate well, meaning how to listen and think critically about what is received, as well as how to form well-reasoned and informed responses. I've noticed the increasing distribution of false nuggets of wisdom, something I too have been guilty of, the regurgitation of something you heard from someone, sometime, somewhere. It's something I consciously stopped doing, repeating things I heard someone else say. I started to ensure that I knew about my topics of discussion, and do you know what happened, I almost stopped talking completely. Not because I didn't know anything, but because so much of our shared talking really is about nothing of great importance.

As I stopped reacting with automated responses that simply popped up out of the deep blue depths of myself, I seemed to start listening in a new way as my level of curiosity spiked. We really do all think we know a little too much about the world and life, for evidence of this look no further than to someone parenting a child, the absolutist stance of some people continues to astound me. Adults spend plenty of time forcing children to be honest and shaming them into submission, sharing their feelings of disappointment at a kid's subconscious and autopiloted 'mistake,' whilst rarely modelling the desired behaviour themselves.

Children don't make mistakes, it was adults who went ahead and labelled the innate resistance to conform that we are all born with as *wrong*, *bad* or *naughty*. I've worked in various mainstream education systems, I'm well versed in child development and have worked with new-born babies all the way through to children aged eleven, and I'll be honest with you, education systems have become nothing more than institutionalised child abuse. I would never dare to say that those who work with our young are abusers, nothing of the sort, it is the system that is abusive and full of an obscene level of neglect.

The devastation of it is that you have a community of beautiful humans who feel inspired to care for the young and take them on journeys of learning and self-expansion, but they are constantly condemned for not being able to work the miracle of making everyone the same. Ultimately, these children are treated as a product, a numbered and labelled statistic that enters a system and appears to matter for a decided period of time. The aim of the game is to shape and manipulate children to behave in line with the preferences of adults; to teach them to regurgitate the information that someone I don't know decided all human minds (of that country) need to know; squash any sense of individuality out of them by devaluing anything that can't be measured and quantified; and make them scared of both success and failure by repeatedly forcing them to sit through various tests that are massively unachievable and meaningless.

To trust any mainstream system of education is foolish and I promise you this... No child of mine will be attending any school that I have stepped foot in.

This seems like an opportune time to share why. You see, I am the most impassioned of teachers, I love your children when they are with me, all equally and for their own essence of individuality. I treasure their words and love to hear what they think, for they have infinite questions that can lead the way of learning. Children are naturally curious, they live with a thirst for the unknown like no other, they live free of words like mistake, right, wrong, discipline, ambition and challenge. They are perpetually interested in the world and its happenings. Yet school ensures that this is all squashed right out of them, the only way it survives is if parents take an active approach towards the expansion of their own child's mind.

I count myself lucky that I seem to have attended school during a period wherein teachers retained some level of autonomy, they had the freedom to choose topics, they had the time to let us follow our own line of inquiry and create projects based on individual interests. We children had time to dance, sing in the choir and create theatrics with teachers, we had *fun*. Upon my return to the UK, I've seen an increasing absence of fun and have determined one main reason as to why: the fun starts with the teachers, but teachers are battered, bruised and exhausted. This once joy-filled calling has become a burden, something to survive the best you can. Most teachers remain in the profession because your children are our passion, there are the rare few who like the holidays more than your children, but you can spot them from a mile off. For the most part, we did not get into this job for any other reason than the kids, believe me, there is no other motivation that could pull you through what has become a gruelling academic year.

So, is there any fun at all you ask? Well, we try our best to squeeze it in between pounding children with all variety of mathematical challenges, stuff that could certainly wait and be left until a solid foundation has been established. Oh, and of course there's reading, where phonics seems all the craze and it has become important to get children to read alien words. Do you know what they are? These are literal gibberish words that make no sense whatsoever, words like *gup, zorp, brip*, created with the intention of testing children's decoding skills. Forget the fact that the whole point of reading is to make meaning from marks presented on a page, what a waste of time that all is. Then there's music of course, well we sing a science song occasionally and these African drummers come in once a year. Art? What's that? Modern foreign languages? Forget it! We in the UK don't even attempt to gift our children with bilingualism in a world that almost demands it.

Forgive me, I'm being facetious, but it's difficult not to be after a decade of trying and failing to find a place in the world that would let me be the teacher I was born to be. I have a natural way with children and it's something not very much valued by the world, but I'll tell you who it is valued by, the kids! I see them, always. I see their individual traits and behaviours that reveal so much, I see their insecurities and fears of being born as not enough to this world, there're those words again, *not enough*. I see their absolute urgency in telling me that they just got a new baby kitten, Dad took them swimming last night or their first tooth fell out. Children have so much to say, but not too many listeners. Maybe people *want* to listen, but feel they have no time, adults are busy, I get it, but darn it, MAKE TIME! You birthed that tiny human, now raise it! And at least try your best to do it properly, which means do what you're always telling your kids to do, tell the truth and learn from your mistakes.

*Don't fear parental failures,
everyone makes them because everyone is a human.*

However, I hear far too often the dismissal of any responsibility to improve with variations of, 'Well, people have been having babies for millennia, can't be that hard,' or, 'No one knows how to raise a child, there is no right or wrong way.' Look, I promised myself I wouldn't swear in this book, so I will say this, that's all total poppycock! And it's also complete rubbish that you know more about children and raising them than I do just because I am not yet a mother. I like to argue that I have the vantage point of depersonalisation, I am more objective *because* I'm not a mother yet and I have learned oh-so-much of what I will never do by observing others. Is that not a fundamental of academic and scientific research, observation?

Shall I tell you the little things I observe that interest me? A child jumping harmlessly whilst waiting for a mum who is shopping and her ordering them to immediately stop enjoying themselves, simply because she wants to shop in peace and pretend they're not there for a moment; a child screaming in a pushchair being left to cry, which, by the way, is a pre-verbal form of communication, they are not whining, they are *communicating a need*; then there's the poor parent with a crying baby on a long-haul flight, made to feel ashamed that their baby is alive and well and doing its thing (although, perhaps the baby is not quite ready to fly and is in the kind of discomfort they shouldn't be, with ears popping and zero comprehension of how to ease their own suffering – just saying). I find people and their reactions interesting, moreover, their absolute absence of self-awareness even more astonishing.

People believe the stories they're told rather than the stories that their bodies tell them, and if we are to talk about protecting our young then why don't we start from birth? Babies cry, people act like that's something scary, but that's only because it's become something to fear. Why do people fear a crying baby, I think it's simply because their minds are so full of what could be wrong that they forget how easy it is to know what is right. I haven't even birthed a child but I already observe my body reacting to the presence of an infant, I am drawn in by their big baby eyes, which are designed by nature to do just that, and feel an instinctive pull to preserve and protect. I have an innate instinct to ruffle their hair, tickle their chin and comfort them when they are sad, but the world tells me even this is wrong now as I am made to feel fearful of other people's perceptions of my natural responses to the presence of children, i.e., I could get sued. I'm not even permitted to offer a congratulatory pat on the shoulder these days.

I see the same fearful shift from our nature can be observed in these poor mothers who listen to any wisdom found in the, 'let your baby self-soothe,' advice. I mean, of course it's proven to work, you break your baby, they learn that no matter how much they protest or cry, no one is coming to offer long-standing comfort. Traditionally, long ago, and perhaps still today in some areas of the world that continue to thrive as connected communities, the common practice was to keep a baby in physical contact with another person for approximately 90% of their young lives. Infants certainly never slept alone or were left to cry periodically in so-called self-soothing distress, it would have disturbed a whole village's sleep cycle for one. I know it is unnatural to leave a baby to cry because my body tells me so, but someone decided my body was wrong, that my impulse to soothe a crying child was unnatural somehow and something to be ignored, not treasured and valued. Something tells me it must have been a man. Yep, it was, I just checked.

Where do stories come from, where did a concept such as 'self-soothe' originate? These are the kind of questions we should be asking. What about another story some collectively believe in these days, the cot? Does a baby need a tiny bed of their own, a little cage? Wow, I never really thought of it like that before, but it is indeed designed with the same architecture as a little prison, built with the similar intention of containing a wild animal. I'm joking of course, a play pen or cot is a practical invention, but one that inspires no trust in one's environment or baby if overused; here we return to the word *balance*. I've seen young ones left in those contained spaces for far too long, yet having already learned the defeat they face in crying about it they have been reduced to an early acceptance of the state of boredom. I see this as the early squashing of one's voice, this kind of prolonged neglect can leave deeply ingrained abandonment issues within one's self as the early lesson is learned, how can anyone love me if they don't even cuddle me when I cry?

This story is of course not true, the child will be treasured and adored, it's not that the parents don't love their child, it is with the greatest of love that they torture themselves into living unnatural behaviour patterns. It is with love that they convince themselves that they are doing the right thing in listening to the advice of a book, a doctor, their own mother, partner or neighbour even. Yet it is not from love that these decisions are born, it is from fear they emerge. I can't stand the sound of a baby crying, not because the noise jars my brain, but because my body instinctively reacts and I must sit with the impulse to provide comfort. I watch people as they cluelessly struggle to manage the situation, mostly because they are quite simply scared of it. Scared of what others think, scared of not knowing what's wrong, scared of this one choice fudging up their child's entire future. The reality is, no one escapes being a bit fudged in some way, so isn't it perhaps better and wiser to face that fact and try our best to teach everybody how to live well as these fudged-up people that we all inevitably become?

Healthy adults make healthy children, for the most part.

The best way to predict in what facets of life your child may be maladjusted is to look to yourself and your partner, identifying any unhealthy patterns that manifest and emerge as a result of an unhealthy core belief or programmed behaviour. For example, do you overeat, overspend or overanalyse? Are you a perfectionist, a workaholic or emotionally unavailable? Do you have healthy rich relationships or experience trouble with others? Do you suffer from social anxiety or drink a little too much? Do you punish yourself with gruelling fitness regimes and count calories or macro nutrients? Are you lazy, spending hours on the couch watching T.V? Everything listed here suggests there is something inside of you that needs looking at, there is some discomfort that exists within that you smother with busyness or numb with a 'chosen' vice.

There are so many things that we could be doing with our days, yet so many of us do the same as one another. Kids don't, kids possess the power to create entire imagined worlds that they can live in and share with one another. Don't we do the same as adults? We just seem to have created a much more miserable and mundane existence than the one we were born to; our appreciation of magic is knocked out of us at a young age as our innocence is stolen by the world, *stolen by adults*. The early sexualisation of children is something I take great issue with, in the name of making money, sex sells after all, the minds of our young are exposed to the unpredictable and they absorb so much that is beyond their ability to process, rationalise and reason. I've watched girls as young as six twerking and little boys thrusting their hips in a discomforting manner. It horrifies me and simply shouldn't be happening.

There is far too much at risk to leave your child unattended in front of either the T.V. or a computer screen, please don't do it, not ever, not unless you are using a controlled and mindful approach. You may be leaving your vulnerable child's mind open to all sorts of influence and even allowing negative behaviour patterns to form as your child's brain morphs and changes in response to the delivered external stimuli. We are creating a generation of tiny addicts, if you leave your child in front of the T.V, a game console or the computer for hours on end, then you're not doing them any favours, you are actually quantifiably causing more harm than good. Do you know the real dangers of the online world? The poison that is designed to be just that and lead your child astray? Did you know that programmers are paid to sequence auto-play features on websites to lead to highly sexualised imagery disguised as child-friendly cartoons? And don't get me started on Peppa Pig, a role model for ill manners and an obnoxious attitude.

So much is designed with your child becoming an adult in mind, if they are already hooked on all this stuff from a young age then big businesses have a much easier time maintaining a consumerist market and unquestioning workforce in an increasingly ethical and moral world. When we talked about balance earlier, well I do believe that one of the main weighing factors tipping the harmonic global scales is greed. Greed made the world what it is, already powerful people who sought more power, more wealth, more security and land, carved up this globe and negotiated terms for us all to live by. The world has outgrown itself and is ready to implode, these times of greed are over, the needs of the many are speaking out over the needs of the few, and our grandest weapons in this fight to save the harmony of this world we call home are self-awareness and knowledge.

It is time for us as a collective to decide upon the knowledge of reality, to find our way towards more agreeable stories, to find value in one another and the way we live, rather than receive anything new and unknown as a threat. Fear divides and weakens us as a people of the world, and it is only together that we will change things for the good of all.

CHAPTER 10

Togetherness

What does togetherness look like? That's a difficult thing to discern if I'm honest, for I don't know that there are too many examples out there in the big wide world visible to the everyday eye. You know, I recently re-entered the workforce here in the UK, that place of work being a primary school, a place that should shroud you in warmth, comfort and a feeling of safety. I mean, that's surely what we're after for our kids, right? Well, it doesn't seem that way to me, there are school improvement officers, coaches, Ofsted inspectors, interfering and self-appeasing governors, as well as local authorities and parents to please, they pull you in every which way. Then there are the two children with severe developmental delays who struggle without any specific or designated adult support; the boy with untold trauma and pain being ignored and his needs set aside, for no one has the time nor resources to manage him; and the shy little girl who barely whispers a word, who remains invisible because she'd have trouble disturbing a bird from its nest. These children are supposed to be my primary focus, yet their true needs seem to be the lowest priority on the rung.

In the five years I spent overseas a lot has changed, there is no money for one, there is one pot for all, on the balancing sheet your child's needs face off with weekly garbage collections, enough said really. Then there is the lockdown drill I had to lead a class of six-year-olds through during our second week of the autumn term, an event that demanded we hide under tables silently for fifteen minutes as a teaching assistant barricaded the door. What are we doing to these poor children? I did not hear of any imminent attacks on the primary schools of England so why the heck are we scaring children? We of course told a story about some stupid cat that was coming to attempt an invasion on the class, thus we must hide, but when is it ever a decent thing to create a fear-based experience for a child this young to live? The school is like a prison anyway with key card entry systems and seven-foot spiked fences, all that's required before we resemble schools on American T.V. are X-ray machines and bag searches.

There are only two schools on this earth where within I

felt utterly safe, nurtured and valued, and that was in the Malaysian jungle. I was a floating teacher responsible for delivering daily English lessons to four-to-seven-year-olds in predominantly Islamic schools and I can say that I've never felt more respected for the individual that I am. I lived some tough and traumatic life experiences whilst under the care of this community and do you know what they did, they loved me in a way I didn't know was possible. What did this look like? They hugged me when I cried and never tried to fix or change me, they didn't provide empty advice or false promises of hope, and they didn't pity me. The strength they observed in me I then got to see in myself, the comfort they offered in allowing my pain gave me a window into self-compassion, and most of all they offered me patience in abundance.

It was at twenty-seven years old that I ventured out onto this unknown adventure and resisted the outspoken fears of others that I would be anything but okay. My whole life I have been a little unusual and I never really understood why until recently, I've figured out that I'm not exactly fearless, it's just I enjoy doing the things that scare me. Perhaps it could be said that I enjoy the feelings of aliveness one gets by stepping into the unknown. Throughout life my intuition has always guided me true and if anyone challenged my capability to carry out an ambition, well, I just pushed harder to prove them wrong. It wasn't the healthiest of patterns, my stubborn perfectionism and inability to fail in the eyes of another cried of a lack of self-worth. However, the shame that bound me to such intense self-critique ensured the discovery of myself as an academic, along with the faith of my one and only mentor, Susanna, she was a pebble of life that continues to ripple into this day.

> *It took a short lifetime to discover myself*
> *and it seems to have happened at a painstaking pace.*
> *It appears I had to first figure out what I wasn't*
> *in order to make way for what I am.*

I think it's possible that community is what allows you to discover who you are and what you're capable of. What is community but another term for a connected group of individuals that make up a part of your external environment? My young life was devoid of a wider community and I only felt the absence of it once I discovered what it was and what it meant to a person to be connected to a world beyond their own insular existence. There is family of course, but community goes beyond that and is a necessary facet of a life lived well. An extended and varied community is what helps a person to explore, expand and discover themselves, the adage I believe is true, *it takes a village.*

It is *The Smurfs* that pop into my head now, the perfect example to illustrate the necessity and beauty of diversity and difference. If everyone were the same in that village then how boring would one of my favourite childhood cartoons have been? I use this to illustrate the richness of a well-balanced and harmonised community, a place where every individual has a purpose and holds value, a world where everyone is accepted exactly as they are. I don't know when we became so scared of being different, when we decided that one size could ever possibly fit all. I guess it might have been when we decided that one size was the answer. Let's go back in time again, to when our present one size was established and set eyes upon, the life of the successful white male. Any deviation from the success-driven narrative of the white male is often misunderstood and therefore feared.

> *Our most crippling curse in this*
> *modern world is the luxury of choice.*

I shared a train ride and visit to the Visual Arts Gallery in Tokyo with a young traveller last year, one of those epic forty-eight-hour mini adventures shared with another whose name you'll never remember, but whose words you occasionally quote to others. Not long after we met and flowed with that easy discourse people on the road to nowhere tend to do, he shamelessly declared the most honest of words, 'As far as I see it, I won the life lottery, I was born a white European male.' This prompted me to contemplate that I may have pulled the second prize on that draw, white European female, for here we both were, stepping through the newly opening global doors of opportunity presented to our generation.

By no means was I born to affluence, I was actually likened to The Flintstones at college on account of my twenty-one-year-old Renault 5. My first car was a dinosaur with no definitive colour, in various lighting it could transform from red to orange to rust, it came with one radio station that favoured country music and retained its original memory foam seats. But as far as I was concerned, it was freedom of a new kind, I couldn't give a hoo-ha what people getting the bus to school thought. And the icing on the cake, the lady selling the car gave it away for free in the end because it needed four new tyres.

My point is, I know the modern world's version of hardship, but to me it was never hardship, it was simply life. Living in the ground floor flat of an old Victorian house came with some colourful experiences; there was the electrically charged wall that would sting when touched; a garden full of fruit trees and stinging nettles that came with the buzzing of bees and flutter of butterflies; the cold unaffordable winters that required us to wear gloves, hats and scarves inside, and to burn the occasional open fire, when we were able to afford the wood.

This could have been something to complain about, but we never did, we laughed a lot instead, and I think travelling the world ensured that it never became a permissible complaint. Comparatively, there is always someone living a worse experience than you, this does not allow the diminishing or vanishing of your own pain, but it does allow for perspective to be gained. All humans experience life in their own way, some people deal with life by crying about it, others by getting angry, and there are those that remain in the bliss of absolute denial.

I attended a New Year's Celebration for the seeing in of 2020, it was in French Brittany that I was introduced to a man of a different energy, something a bit on the darker side. I know darkness when I feel it, let me make it clear what I mean by this, I know the feeling of a person who has lived challenging experiences that border on or surpass being unbearable to the human form and psyche. Perhaps I know it because I've lived it. Anyway, this guy, let's call him Jean, was identified to me as the firecracker, the one people are wary of, I listen to offerings like this but tend to make my own mind up about people. As with so many men who are

FAITH

mistaken, this guy had a gentleness about him and acknowledged my existence more than many others.

I sat next to him at dinner and although we had no lingual connection, we enjoyed a happy time. Perhaps it is those of us who must hide ourselves and remain somewhat invisible because the world rejects our natural state of being who are able to see one another. I recall the moment that my pain separated me from the world, when the straw that broke the camel's back came crashing down with untold force. I remember the crippling pain awake in my chest cavity as a sound I'd never before heard escaped my mouth. Despair. Agony. *Reality.* The death of innocence.

As the stroke of midnight approached, I was invited out to the back garden where fireworks were to be ignited against the backdrop of an old village church. With what I thought were twenty minutes to spare, I zipped to the bathroom and upon exiting stopped to chat with my friend Kevin, who was talking his way into the new year with Jean (unbeknown to me, the fireworks had already begun). The conversation was intense, so I lingered aside, I love intense (way more than fireworks). They were in fact discussing Jean's tendency towards aggression, his quick temper that fires up when triggered by a perceived injustice. This stranger was living with visible agony, I saw a deep-rooted shame of himself, reflected back and confirmed by the judgement of the world around him. It occurred to me to ask Kevin to translate the following, 'In another time and place the man you are would have been valued and respected as a warrior. Do not be ashamed of yourself, your way just doesn't belong to today.'

It's true, is it not? Not so long ago the reactions of a strong and powerful man would have made him a sound soldier and potential leader. But today men are being asked to quickly change and alter their projected ego to reflect more the desired stories shown to us by popular culture and the like. This is neither fair nor realistic. Just as men need to find better, less disruptive ways to express their frustrations, so too do women need to learn to harness their emotional rollercoasters into effective communication strategies. We throw our emotional rubbish in the other direction far too easily and often take little responsibility for our own unconscious automatic reactions. If you don't like something it is up to you to figure out why and deal with it, it is up to you to tolerate whatever is unpleasant about a situation or remove yourself from it. It's your job to set your own boundaries, I'll just wager a guess that no one ever explicitly taught you how to. No, me neither.

Boundaries and healthy, two words that, when thrown together, can mean the transformation of your own life and self. What are healthy boundaries? I'll guess Jean can't identify his, he wouldn't be putting himself in situations wherein he allows them to be crossed if so. I see so much sadness in people who feel misunderstood by the world, those who can't maintain enough control over themselves to allow people to get close enough to meet the real them. I realise that this was me for such a long time, living with subtle less disruptive patterns, but patterns that kept me guarded and safe from the world, nonetheless. I think my absolute interest in humans has been my greatest defence, preferring the asking of questions to the answering of them. That was until I met Phillip.

Listening to someone allows them to change their own life.

Phil became a good friend of mine, the best I'd ever had in fact, up to that point at least. What made him so? His ability to listen without moving to fix, the bucket loads of empathy that let him see a person in great need of telling her stories and the integrity to keep it all to himself. I learned what it meant to listen well when I became in need of a person who could do so. Prior to living that experience, I had thought myself a dandy listener, willing to absorb the sorrows and woes of another for hours at a time, at a young age becoming the shoulder many had cried on. I thought this made me a good person and someone of compassion and empathy, but I was wrong. I gave far too much advice to make me a good listener, then the other end of the problem was the person who never took the advice. I would listen, help them feel temporarily better after becoming their emotional rubbish bin, try to provide healthy steps forwards, only to repeat it all the following week.

The mistake I was making was thinking that another person's problems were mine to fix. When we look to alter the lives of others, is it simply because we are avoiding the changes that would be welcome in our own? There was only one thing I had control over throughout those years of chronic unhealthy listening and that was whether I did it or not. Only I had the power to break these cycles that contributed zero positive energy to my world, but I felt ashamed to, in the face of another's suffering I have never been able to turn a blind eye. But much of the time we live in a loop, repeating the same nature of complaint or even more horrifyingly, repeating the *exact same* complaint for years on end.

Have you ever watched someone relive an unpleasant tale from their past, seen how their energy can shift and return to the negative vibe of the moment it was lived? Internally their reality alters and they're back there, reliving the same emotions, thoughts and reactions as the very first time it happened. Heck, they may have even fed that little thought demon with more narrative and drama to make it all more deliciously juicy. The mind doesn't like to let things go, it likes to be right and justified and it bases this on what it's programmed with.

Reality is relative to perception.

There are billions of people on this earth all experiencing life in their own unique way, and to observe that reality only exists when you perceive that it does, the question arises whether the world exists without your perception of it. I think it all might exist, but what becomes absent is any awareness of its existing. Without anything existing in the mind of the human, without the realms of words and labels, is anything real? What is definably real anyway? I believe that it's beyond these words that we move closer to reality, when we strip away all the human-made meanings we might just come a little closer to the world of God. It is a world free of words that lives freely together, for words create every fear, barrier, block and boundary that stands in the way of you and The Other. Togetherness is perhaps what we find when we let go of ourselves.

CHAPTER 11

Letting Go

Letting go, not so many of us know how to do this, our bodies know how, we just don't let them because the world makes us forget. Letting go is what we were built to do, letting go is what emotion is all about, but the world fears feeling, so it rests in the comfortable realms of reacting. To feel demands the courage to allow the pain to arise and then to pass. To be uncomfortable is to admit that reality is not what we'd wish it to be and to face where any arising stories come from that say it should be otherwise. Why do we need things to be different? This is the question that stands between you and letting go. What is it in the here and now that gives you such unease and why?

There is a happy experiment that I like to live, especially at those times when it feels as though the world is about to cave in and finally steal my sanity. You see, I've never been one

FAITH

for meditating and much like a child, if I don't want to do something you will not make me. To me meditation is boring and an utter waste of my time, and for all the spiritual seeking that I lived I never once succumbed to the belief that to find peace I had to sit still and surrender to myself. I'd argue that meditation cannot be practiced without a degree of self-awareness and vice versa, I don't know that one can exist without the other. As for me, I came to live in a state of constant *active* meditation as I became aware of observing my Self and its happenings in relation to the world and various lived experiences. I became my own fascination and with that the concept of meditation became a little less boring.

So, back to that experiment; I like to sit around and notice the outside world sometimes rather than focus solely on my own inside one, now this makes for an interesting meditation. It's intriguing to sit somewhere quiet, perhaps with the twitter of birds and rustle of leaves, especially in those darker more challenging moments of life, and take note that not a single thing is happening around you at that given time. When you tune into your senses and explore your immediate world you become more connected to it somehow and draw the mind away from dwelling in the pain of the past and anxieties of the future. For the briefest of moments, you feel safe from your pain, you feel free of its

LETTING GO

grip as you allow the peace of the present to fill you up.

This is no quick-fix miracle by any means, but it is a moment of respite to be found in a life of received and perceived chaos. To sit still and meditate felt like imagined torture to me, when really, all traditional meditation is trying to do is get you to sit still and stop avoiding yourself for a moment. But I believe there are many other ways to stop avoiding oneself, more productive, no less scary, but certainly more active ways, such as physical activity and the arts. When I refer to the arts, much to the chagrin of my good friend, I am talking about various non-verbal and verbal forms of self-expression and communication. He likes to think that the visual arts dominate and are what make a true artist, arrogant sculptor that he is, yet I see art as a lived experience, a way of connecting two selves by way of more abstract means of communication.

In the creating of art there is a letting go, a piece of oneself left in a moment. But for art to be an expression of self it must be seen, heard and valued; it has to matter somehow. We live in a world where things only matter if someone else permits them to, from the very beginning we are told whether our work is up to scratch, whether we hold any uniqueness or grand potential in a world that fosters neither. It has become increasingly apparent that the only person a thing need matter to is oneself. I wonder if it is in every corner of the world that adults ask children a variation of, 'Well, if he jumped off a bridge, would you do the same?' Our inability to think and tendency to follow is there from the get-go, along with those inner core values and beliefs that have us impulsively acting out against our better judgement. After all, we all know better, yet these same playground problems persist into adulthood, easily found in the workplace and amidst social settings.

Do we ever really grow up? How many of us are actually adults? Let's face it, if children are acting in an unsavoury manner then they learned it from one primary source, the adults around them, and perhaps poorly chosen T.V. and other media sources. If your child swears, it's on you. If your child sets fires, it's on you. If they bite, scream, scratch or remain painfully insular—it's on you! This may make you feel angry, but that's only because I'm touching on something living inside of you that you already feel angry about, whether you've admitted it to yourself or not. This feeling does nothing but tell you something about yourself and the situation. Don't be scared to go there, for the sake of both you and your child. It makes you the best possible parent you can be, a willingness to look honestly at yourself and to work towards change based on what you see.

To look at your own life can lead to a deep sense of grief as you gaze upon squandered years wasted in an idle stance.

When I awoke to the reality of myself, a visual awoke in my mind's eye, a timeline of my life appeared as a misty veil of trauma was lifted so that I might see with clarity the truth of the life I had lived. Recalling the lies I told myself brings an unease to my body as I remember the shock of realising that I wasn't exactly who I thought I was. This calls for an example; I was single for a little over thirteen years, something I had been at semi-peace with. I had stories attached to this aspect of my life: I was independent, didn't need a man, or anyone for that matter, I wasn't ready to settle down, plus, I knew from the outset whether I liked someone or not, right?

There were other strange things that manifested from my deep-seated belief that I was worthless and undeserving of love. You see, I wasn't just single, I hadn't gone on a date for over a decade either, men just didn't ask me. All of this certainly reinforced the ugliness and repulsion I felt towards myself, for the world certainly seemed to confirm everything I thought and felt. Why didn't men ask? Well, I have only just come to realise that it was because I gave them nothing to go on, I was a person of no reaction, that's why I didn't often trigger people and was quite the adept chameleon. But not reacting meant not connecting too. And so, I think men did come onto me, I just never felt anything to react to, numb as I was. Some males, people I considered friends, declared their love for me at various times and I simply dismissed them with my own easy disbelief, punching their arm as I muttered, 'Don't be silly. Of course you don't love me.' This lack of love for myself meant I couldn't even fathom the possibility that another could love me, even when they told me so.

What we believe is what we perceive.

These were big stories, clearly, massive blocks to connection, intimacy and relationship. It wasn't just that I couldn't be intimate, it also seemed that the men I attracted and allowed to get close-adjacent didn't end up being diamond geezers. I have become so grateful for my body and its defence mechanisms, they protected me from a lot over the years. As I entered young adulthood I was welcomed to the world of coupled connection with physical and emotional abuse, it took as little as seven months for me to break free of these patterns, promising myself at sixteen years old that I would never again be treated in such a manner. It seems my way of ensuring this meant shutting down all possible intimate threats in the blink of an eye, no one was getting close to me any time soon.

Sixteen years it took before someone came along who was bold enough to blast through the walls that I had lived protected by for so long. Can you imagine the reactions awaiting that poor soul? Navigating the mess that was my inner world at that time proved a feat and a half, one that I barely survived with my dignity intact. The fears that existed within manifested externally as projected stories of insecurity, confusion and mistrust. I knew enough of what was going on, my past was surfacing and interfering with my present, yet again. But it proved challenging trying to explain that my unfathomable reactions were not in fact the real me, just fears that lived inside of me that needed to come out so that they might fade away for good. Living with a fear of being misunderstood, something that often causes accidental pain, I have always tried to explain myself to others if I upset them. This is perhaps one of the driving forces behind the journey to understanding my own complexity with such rigor and depth, but also a part of my nature that pushes people away.

People tend to fall into two categories:
those who reject help, and those who accept too much of it.

I think to truly let go means first acknowledging that your reaction has nothing at all to do with the other person, or any other triggering cause. If you have a fear of intimacy then it's no good accusing the other of being smothering or needy, which they may well be, but only if you allow it with poorly communicated boundaries. If you feel smothered, it's because you feel undeserving of affection and love. If you are needy, it's because you are scared that this love presently filling a void existing since childhood will disappear, as you too are trapped in the belief that no one will ever love you enough to stick around. Unfortunately, it is the fear of the thing happening that so often results in the eventuality of it. We reject the very love we crave in the same moment that we reject ourselves and the truth of who we are. So long as we point the finger in the other direction we remain stuck, doomed to face the same cycles of predicable patterning and perpetual pain.

So, what's the answer? How do we let this stuff go? How do we fix ourselves? Here's the funny part, we do not move to fix or change a thing, we simply accept things exactly as they are, *especially* ourselves. If you dislike the feeling of physical closeness because the word *smothering* comes to mind, recognise why and be uncomfortable for a little while, I promise you that it will soon pass, even if soon means a few months or even years. Change takes time. If you are needy as heck and panic every time your partner leaves the room to go to the bathroom, take a breath and talk to yourself.

Acknowledge that your absentee father left you with some subconscious baggage to deal with, but that the guy in the bathroom had nothing to do with it.

> *Own your pain, own the discomfort,*
> *for on the other side of it lies freedom.*

The only way is through, there is no avoiding the uncomfortable parts of yourself should you choose to proceed with self-work, it is the entire point of it, to look at what's standing between you and a more fulfilling life. It's much easier to make up stories as to why your finances are a mess, why you are perpetually single or why you can just never seem to lose weight. Reality is always much harder to face because it means taking a good honest look in the mirror and admitting to yourself whether you like what you see, and if you don't, taking ownership of that. The way to falling in love with yourself is to first see those parts of yourself that are unloved and shine a little light on them. If you have a fear of fitness, one I lived with for a time, it comes from a shame of not being good enough. Just watch as fear tells you how embarrassed you'll be, how terribly you'll hold up the group or how there's no point anyway as nothing's ever worked before. All these thoughts ever stop you from doing is living the life you deserve.

FAITH

The best way to dispel an illusionary thought, in my opinion, is to do the thing anyway and see if the voice was right. More often than not these self-limiting voices tend to diminish rather quickly once proven wrong, which they almost always are. Dancing, my body's one true love, something I loved to do all my life, yet a thing I was always too scared to expand on, was where I lived evidence of this. I remember my tentative arrival at a one-on-one Latin dance class, I was about to live a dream I'd had since childhood, perhaps spawned from the hours I spent watching Patrick Swayze twirl girls in pink dresses and John Travolta hop around on car bonnets, yet all I felt was defeated. It was crazy, I knew I could dance, my bedroom mirror told me so, yet I had an inward certainty of being met with shame, humiliation and embarrassment. What a relief it was to find these myths and legends of my own making were disproven with haste. It wasn't long before I was speed boating through the mangroves three times a week on a local busboat for my two-hour sessions, I was officially hooked.

Over time, I watched the voice in my head change and right alongside it a beautiful story started to form as I fell in love with my own body. It wasn't that I just started enjoying the way it looked and moved, it was that it existed with these in-built intelligences that once trusted, once unleashed, seemed to take on a mind of their own. As I continued to step into my fears, including twirls, twists and lifts, I began to notice how my body aligned with my mind, in less fear-based moments I would move freely as I trusted my 3D form to know what to do. When uncertainty struck, it was already game over as the mind interjected and the body became tense and contracted, frozen ever-so-slightly by fear. Just as the energy of a river is free to flow until it meets a dam, fear presents much the same blockage for the flow of a body exploring the motion of dance.

The whole body's mechanics are built around the form of infinity, the joining of which can be found at your sternum, or solar plexus. It's incredible to experience how your extended leg and pointed toes require no attention at all, form is of course important, but the movement itself originates from the torso; as you internally manipulate your core with the visual of infinity at work, your leg will move itself. This had me in hysterical giggles as I moved in awe of my own body, a feeling that only intensified as I realised those beautiful arm movements of dancers were made all the more accessible with this knowledge too. It was a massive key that unlocked something magical and unbeknown to me.

A nifty way of letting go is to learn new things, anything, the mind can only believe something if you continue to allow it to do so, the best thing you can do is contradict it.

FAITH

The more you contradict it the more you become living proof of its own lies and the less it seems to chatter and interfere. The thing is, to do the scary thing one must first figure out what they wish to do that they are afraid of, for some this may be easy to determine, for others less so after years of hiding from themselves and the world and pretending to enjoy adulthood. In this case, the best point of reference is childhood, those short-lived years on earth when you were allowed to choose and follow your own interests and passions. Otherwise, if you are fully disconnected from your once original self, enjoy the discovery of yourself, getting to know what you like and dislike, and work from there. If you have a fear of even this then you certainly have some work to do and even that will scare some of you, please don't let it.

> *The thought of something is almost
> always worse than the reality of it.*

The mind has a great way of making something out of nothing and is especially great at conjuring up potential negatives. There is a deep-seated shame built into our human programming that tells us not to aim too high, that there is something wrong in loving ourselves, that speaking well of ourselves is egocentric and arrogant. I beg to differ, we are quite quick to diminish ourselves out loud, so where does the fault lie in admitting to your own worth and value? The more we say this out loud the better, for we give other people permission to celebrate themselves in return. Children are great at this, it's a favourite moment of mine when a child unashamedly produces a beautiful scribble that they go on to declare their love of. Why do they love it? Because they made it, in that moment their little heart and soul was full of intent and this scribble was the result of it. I wonder what reaction I might get if I started happily handing people my perfectly imperfect little doodles, probably a response far removed from, 'Oh wow! That is beautiful my little darling, what were you thinking about when you drew it?'

We stop delighting in one another, is this simply because we are fearful of the mirror The Other presents to us? The Other is often easier to look at than ourselves, but any harsh external criticisms we may have are simply reflections of something in existence within. Anytime an experience is distasteful or classified as unpleasant by your system, don't just blindly accept that it's because there is a problem, something is only ever a problem if your mind makes it so. There are no problems, remember, only the stories your mind tells. If a situation brings a feeling inside of you that is difficult to allow, that's when it's ever more important to

FAITH

allow it, for it is in the allowing that the letting go happens. Every single experience is made up of a complex series of chemical and physiological happenings and reactions, a situation without a determinable beginning or end, it's the unknown moving in continuous waves of energy, a whole body of matter always connected, always combined, always one.

Can you allow the thought to creep in that you are neither separate from this world nor really a part of it? Can you allow the thought that *you* are the world, in the sense that you *are* nature? Just as an ant is born to a colony, we are born to society, just as elephants grieve and revisit a grave, so too do we feel the loss of a loved one. The way in which we experience life may be different from many other species of animal, but there is no denying that every single way of life lived is to be revered and valued. Existence is the miracle we've all been searching for folks. To live is the greatest gift we'll ever be given, it's only that our minds were never taught to believe it, our minds were programmed with other stories. We sit around praying for miracles, waiting for an external force to prove itself, when it quite laughably already did, *it created you*.

CHAPTER 12

Change

The world would have you believe that you are powerless. It would have you blindly accept the fate you were born to, don't. We all hold the power within to change our lives and the place to start is with yourself. It would have been easy for me to get angry, to blame others for the state of my life, but with love in my heart it was forgiveness I sought. Forgiving others meant first forgiving myself and accepting my fate as being in no one else's hands but my own. It's time to stop blaming the world for our state of affairs. It's okay to feel angry about things, or disappointed, just as children do, the part we've forgotten is how to let go and jog on. What's the other thing children do well? They cry.

Crying has a bad rap and I don't know why. I've thought about it extensively and observed our patterns as a species around this in-built human mechanism designed to release the energy of a lived moment as salty flowing water. Tears rock as far as I'm concerned, tears allow my pain to flow from the internal to the external world, as do the occasional burp or yawn funnily enough. Like I said, our bodies are smart, they know exactly what to do, we just don't know how to let them. From the onset of birth we are told to stop crying, with intended silencing disguised as a soothing, 'Shhh! Shhh! Shhh! Little one.' What does, 'Shhh!' mean in any language other than, 'Please stop making that sound and be quiet'? An adult's own discomfort of a given sound inspires them to stop the source of the discomfort, the crying baby, rather than soothe the child in a more nurturing way that meets the actual need being presented. Being someone who has found crying to be an essential element of emotional release, my motto is:

You've got to feel it to heal it.

There is no skirting around the things from the past that linger in your being, they are there whether you like it or not, whether you accept it or not, but simply because you were not provided with the tools to let them go. If anything, you were born with innate tools that the world oppressed you into forgetting, I'm here to help you remember. Some might say that some women are good at crying, but I beg to differ, being one myself I have experienced the painful loops of suffering that heightened sensitivity can bring. For many years I did indeed cry a lot, but more for others than myself. I have felt the pain of the world, of *The Other*, rather intensely all my life.

At six years old I would come home from school and cry for the disabled boy who was born with half an arm, or feel dismayed any time a black person on T.V. was presented as anything less than what they are, a whole and worthful human. I didn't understand the world and its pain, I could never comprehend how others could so blindly cause the suffering of another without even seeming to see the damage their words or actions had. I was in a continual state of devastation as the world did nothing but present the ugliness and selfishness of humankind, all born from the same intrinsic primal fear and need to survive. Up to this point survival has been built around a model of selfishness, a mindset or *either-or*. Why can't we all survive? Isn't it time to admit defeat for everyone, and in that defeat find the victory we all truly seek—peace? There is only one place for peace to be sought, within, it is the only place one need venture. The same might be said for freedom, about which comes our next poem. I hope you find it reflective...

FAITH

Free Yourself

A life of aimless wanderings,
Floating from here to there,
Searching for answers in the external,
When all I need know,
Lay right here.

Fearless, wild and free,
We are born unto this world,
Yet in mind, body and soul,
We are bound,
To the story that unfurls.

Born to place, position, people,
We step into a tale unknown,
No choice in who we are to be,
Trapped by that which we think we know.

Security is found in the story,
In this familiar sense of self,
A whole world in your mind,
Stored in chapters on a dusty shelf.

It's time to clean for spring,
To burn the books of old,
No new chapter pre-written,
No dream of the story to unfold.

Each day, each hour, each moment,
Is a presence of love to be lived,
So free yourself from the story,
And embody this beautiful gift.

Burning the books of old, that's what all of this is about really, isn't it? Throwing away the knowledge and stories of the past that no longer serve us as a humanity. There are too many to count, too many fear-based conflicts that exist in our beautiful world. When we take ourselves into the beauty of nature, we reveal our own. In a growing flower we see no fault, in its wilting and discolouring petals we allow its natural course of life to eventuate. The thing we do not realise is that there is no death of the flower, only a transformation of energy. Just as a caterpillar spins its chrysalis and emerges a butterfly, never being conscious of its own doing so, so too do we evolve and transform beyond our own comprehension, we just like to play pretend at understanding it all.

FAITH

All the conflict in the world can be traced back to early playground patterns, the polarities of *I'm right* and *you're wrong*; then there're the cool boys and the sensitive 'crybabies', I don't even like writing this phrase. I can't imagine the pain of being an emotional male whose tears flow easily, I'm sure this must be knocked out of so many by secondary school. The one and only reaction that should be lived when a person cries is to let them, hugs can help, but those of the right kind, those with a safe and trusted person have the power to open the floodgates and aid another in release. The same can be said for letting another person feel and be angry, but unfortunately, we are as scared of other people's emotions as we are of our own. Why do we fear what we are?

I have been given the most patronising of hugs, the kind where the person stands in all their unknowing self-righteousness, never realising that they are bound by many of the same fears I am releasing in those tears. And then there are those who tell me to stop crying; when I cry people think there is something wrong with me, there's really not, I'm just feeling for a moment. As I lost the gift of verbal communication upon entering the Malay-speaking jungle, I became more attuned to what children actually need and in turn, to what I needed too. You see, my ability to provide words of comfort, words of fixing and changing, were removed and I had to simply let children cry and feel their own feelings. It was a beautiful learning, all these children required from me was a shared moment of safety, comfort and release. I think togetherness is perhaps essential to the release of pain sometimes, I don't quite know why, but it lingers there as a curious puzzle to solve.

Together is how we survive this life, it always has been, but what does together mean when our need of one another no longer determines our survival? An isolated mind is dangerous, I should know, without other people around to challenge your perception of reality it is possible to remain stuck in your own delusions and a world of fantasy. Fantastical thinking is more common in us all than you might think, the dream car, the dream house, the next lotto ticket that you have a good feeling about, they are all fantasies. Daydreams reveal so much of our subconscious mind and programming, I, for one, was unable to even fantasize happiness in my world for years, my imagination conjured up nothing but predictable pain for me.

> *You see, predictions are born from the known,*
> *any projection of the future is likely fuelled*
> *by that which you've already lived.*

The mind is a stubborn beast, which when already

programmed takes a saint to slay. It is impossible for us to change ourselves without anything but an iron stomach, the road is long and the fight within yourself brutal. There is nowhere to hide once you find yourself broken through the illusion of who you thought you were. Running from ourselves manifests in so many ways and there are plenty of books and Googled pages to find ways to help yourself shift toward a better future, but the reality is that most changes we make are small and take time to permeate throughout our lives. The best chance this world has at change is for adults to face the truth of themselves and make way for our children to become the change we all yearn for and seek. Can we trust our children to guide us and finally flip the adage, *age is wisdom*, in the appropriate direction?

Children are the future, I can't think who said it, but someone did, yet we contain them to a past we already know. It is a rare parent I have met who wishes to replicate their own childhood for their offspring, yet far too many end up doing so. Personal change is not required to protect your child from your own parenting, but a development of self-awareness is. It is in knowing the parts of yourself that you do not wish to pass down that you prevent it from happening, denial, blissful ignorance and shame simply ensure it. Brave are the parents who sway from the norm, the mothers who breastfeed in public, the fathers who listen to their children, those who choose to home school. I think trusting one's own child is perhaps the bravest move, trusting their own little intuitive model to seek and explore likes and preferences, to detect danger and potential harm. It is the interpretation of these happenings that they need assistance with.

So, what are we to tell children when they cry? How are we to nurture the increasingly angry little boy or draw out a painfully silent girl full of shyness? First thing we tell them is that whatever they feel is okay, that there is nothing wrong, it's just that their body is reacting to whatever is happening. It is with the questions we ask that we shape and guide the experiences these tiny humans live. Our immediate response of, 'What's wrong?' when faced with the distress of a child only tells them that whatever just happened must have been wrong, thus shaping their emerging tale and tainting any follow-up dialogue. One of the greatest irritations in the classroom is a lack of harmony, the tiny disruptions such as poked-out tongues, the, 'He looked at me funny,' moments, or when children feel betrayed and dismayed as they tell me, 'Robin told me we're not friends anymore.'

Children already rely on one another for validation of various kinds, so too do they seek meaningful connections and feel the loss of said connections when they are disrupted or removed. But no one gives me the time to help them understand that it's okay, no one lets me teach the magic of sorry and reparative power of forgiveness. No one lets me teach these children how to let go and feel safe in their little bodies and minds. On the contrary, people actually force me to work against the needs of the tiny humans, they put me in uncomfortable and ethically questionable positions, all in the name of achievement and standards.

I despise the education system for failing our young so terribly, the research is done, the findings are sound, we've got it totally wrong. Can we accept this yet? Can our governments relinquish any perverse belief that they know what they are doing in this regard and hand it over to the people with experience and those who, more importantly, *care*? The people who work with your children are the ones who know them. Can you trust us? Can you listen to the truths we speak and support the changes needed that seek nothing but a nurturing, stimulating and expansive series of experiences for your child? If we throw out the book and collapse the system tomorrow, will you bring your children to school and trust us to deliver what they need, all the while making sure we still get paid in the face of our active and very professional rebellion?

No one knows what's right, not totally and never with 100% certainty, anyone who claims to know something for sure is living in a state of self-denial and fear, don't waste your time. The mind is stubborn and you will never change that of another's without a fight, so it's wise not to bother trying, unless the person in question matters a great deal to you. We also have no right to try and change another, having gone into some of the things that keep us trapped in loops and cycles, I would never, in awareness, force another to go there themselves. Although, a little healthy poking and prodding never hurt anyone, yet the hard truths are best saved for intuitive moments of release. I'm sure we've all lived a moment when a near stranger or even a signpost has offered the exact words we needed to hear in a time of need.

The world works in mysterious ways, and up to now any occurrence that lay beyond the comprehension of humankind has been labelled as miraculous or given an attached story that could somehow be likened to the myths and legends of old.

> *I prefer to call it, The Unknown,*
> *rather than make up stories about it all.*

In dissecting particular threads throughout time, we are able to see the emergence from lower levels of ignorance. The evolution of medicine, something expanding alongside our understanding of human physiology and beyond, is a

FAITH

fascinating thread, people once having believed that blood pumped in an infinite flow from the heart and simply disappeared at your head, toes and fingertips. History amuses me, humans amuse me. Their absolute capacity to believe what they are told is mind blowing and I do believe blasts open what we think we know about ourselves. This is the first thing we must acknowledge if this human world has a chance at changing before it destroys itself, that we are basic, as basic as they come.

We are as simple as computers, the closest replica humans have made of themselves, artificial intelligence is something people have come to fear and an entire stream of popular culture is driven by this fascination. Isn't it ridiculous that we waste any more time creating things we must be scared of? Can we get to grips with the dangers to ourselves and our young that we have already created and slow down on this incessant ego-driven need for more, faster and bigger? We know so much already, why don't we start fuelling the evolution of *applicable knowledge*, that which improves the life of each individual?

But back to being computers, we like to think ourselves complex, but it's only ever as simple as this: be born to earth; live some experiences that programme you with beliefs, judgements and an ultimate life blueprint; live believing you have choices and free will, when you ultimately spent most of your time running around in circles, only to die before that promised pot of gold appeared. I find the contemplation of free will fascinating and I think it perhaps exists beyond the existence of stubborn day-to-day patterning. I think free will belongs to self-awareness and a mindful approach to life. Free will lives within the realms of conscience, reasoned thought and action, not a place too many of us dwell in for any extended period of time.

CHAPTER 13

The Illusion of Choice

Did you choose your latest haircut? Did you create the thought of it, or did you blindly absorb it from a media source? Let's take my latest fringe, that's right folks, my five-year-old bangs are back! But let me think now, did I choose my bangs? How did the forehead evolve from an uncovered state to being covered with a now falling fringe? Well, there was the emergence of that forehead wrinkle I mentioned earlier, but even prior to that I had doted over Zooey Deschanel's locks for years, although convincing myself the look wasn't for me. Couldn't have been more wrong by the way, I've been rocking these things, even after moments of 'new bang arrogance' when I presumed a trim would be a doddle to do myself (it wasn't). I have to say, I rather enjoy my childlike moments, when I get to shrug something off that might usually have presented as a bother, when I get to think, 'Ah, it's only a little wonky in a few places and that wedge cut at the side is perfectly fine.'

So, did I get my bangs to further hide time showing itself on my face? Did I get bangs because I finally had the courage to follow a look I'd loved for ages? Or even, did I get bangs because I associated them with the character from *New Girl,* Jess, whose eternal optimism and loyal group of friends were as enviable as her hair? Who knows, is the simultaneous question and answer. There is no telling why, at thirty-two years old on a road trip to Cornwall, I awoke one morning and decided Plymouth was the city in which my bangs would be born. It's also possible that being rejected by a man who I thought loved me, as well as discovering myself and my new identity, post jungle, also contributed to this change. But was it *chosen*? When was the actual choice made? The first time I appreciated the aesthetics of bangs? The first time I imagined getting them myself? The moment I booked the appointment? Or only when I let the scissors snip?

I told you before, I don't have many answers, but there are plenty of questions that offer fruitful contemplations and blow apart any answers I thought I might have landed on. Answers are comfortable, our minds like them. But I no longer know whether our minds like answers because that's how they work or whether we taught them to do so, I'm inclined to go with the latter.

> *Children are fantastical thinkers,*
> *their imaginations capable of believing in anything.*

The other day I flipped a scarf over my face as I embodied the role of an alien who was lost in our school, he'd crash landed a few weeks before and we've been talking and writing about it ever since. The point is, after my Oscar-worthy performance as this obscure nameless alien, the kids played at trying to trick me. As I re-entered the classroom, they told me excitedly about the alien visit I'd just missed and asked me what I knew about it. As soon as I acknowledged knowing something I could have only known if I were present at the alien Q&A, their collectively keen eye observed and declared, 'See, it *was* you. *You* were the alien!' Adorable, right?

Sometimes I question whether we take advantage of children's naivety and easy trust and misuse it for our own pleasure and amusement. Although this kind of work is well-researched and a sound context is established wherein the children's minds feel safe to explore the unknown and unpredictable, it is still possible to abuse the power found in the absolute trust of children. Children listen to and absorb everything, every vibration that leaves your mouth will reach

FAITH

them in some form or another, be that simply on an energetic level or as actual and comprehensible words. Children are not as limited as adults might think, just because children cannot perceivably comprehend and discuss an experience does not mean they go untouched by it. On the contrary, children experience every living moment as fully as we do, if not more so.

Let's take the existence and subsequent death of Santa as an example, the jolliest of men who brought them such joy for years dies in an instant when his existence altogether is dispelled as a myth. I watch parents as their children begin to probe for the truth, perhaps because of something they heard, or maybe reasonable and rational thought are just around the corner. Some parents wisely throw the question back with another, allowing their child to find their own way to the truth in good time, others deny their suspicions with assurances and convincing, thus ensuring that *they* get one more Christmas with Santa in the house. There is a selfishness to these stories, for I don't think it was a child that created the story of Santa. Any stories children create we prefer to label as wrong or untrue when they don't fit into the compartments that we have ready and waiting.

Saint Nicholas, now there's a story with Christmas at the heart of it, a generous man who gave to the needy and shared his wealth among others. But that's not the story we tell, is

THE ILLUSION OF CHOICE

it? No, this big guy Santa, now, he monitors you right alongside your parents, sometimes he even communicates with them behind your back, and he records everything you do each year to decide if you are worthy of his gifts (all made off the back of slave labour by the way, those poor brainwashed elves know no different). It all seems very *behavioural theory* to me, positive and negative conditioning, reward and punishment, right and wrong, and is there a distinction felt between being worthy of Santa's toys and worthy of your parent's love? In these stories of old there are no intrinsic values encoded into the delivery, there is no purpose to the story other than to fuel control, commerce and consumerism.

> *At the end of the day, it is a lie we tell*
> *without any thought as to why,*
> *or any question as to the harm it might do.*

The difference between the make believe and imagined worlds of children and a concept such as Santa is that one is of their own creation and the other is a lie they are told, a long-standing conspiracy that results in an abrupt end to magic. The very thing we treasure in children we go on to destroy by claiming it as our own to enjoy. My mother is sometimes dismayed by my thinking, horrified by the thought of her future grandchildren being deprived of Father Christmas. In my aim to please, I suggested that it might perhaps be okay if this lived experience were somehow used to illustrate, 'See, you'll believe anything you're told. Let's look at why and become aware of that aspect of yourself.' This wouldn't be my preferred choice, I'd rather explore the concept of reality with any children I might have and dispel any illusionary need for me to make up the very magic that exists anyway.

I don't want my children to have to escape reality to find contentment and joy, I don't want reality to be a place of hard truths and painful internal conflicts. Better than the gift of Santa is the gift of acceptance. To raise a child with an awareness of reality and all it comprises is the greatest gift a parent could bestow, to help a little one grow with an appreciation of themselves and learn how to live expansively and fully is all we should be contemplating. Every person reading this deserved the same and I'm sorry if a safe and expansive childhood was not your lot, mine neither, but the thing is, that reality exists for far fewer people than you might imagine. I have only one friend I would deem as 'healthy,' in all my searching, it is only one person I have met who embodies what it means to expand with ease, awareness and joy.

I have often questioned that by the laws of attraction this

may well be a limited pool of subjects, like meets like, and I could be deemed somewhat unhealthy on the spectrum of measurable human patterns and behaviours. But I don't like this word, I'm actually throwing it away right now. What does it mean to be *healthy*? Why it means to fit into a box of course. Did you know that there are over one hundred and thirty decided personality types and disorders? Do you know I lost count of how many potentially describe me? We like labels, but by golly, why do we insist on labelling ourselves through such harsh and judgmental lenses? With everything that the world says must be *right* about you, it immediately sets a contrast for you to know what must be *wrong*, that same model from childhood persists.

I have been horrified upon my return to the UK to see the state of commercial television. It is a pure and utter bombardment of fear-based programming and I'll break down some of the stories I see for you. Now, please remember this is just from a few advertisements, it doesn't even begin to touch on the T.V. shows and films being projected every single day into the homes of families and the like...

Example 1

Projected stimulus: Anything dietary or fitness related.

Intended message: Your body looks wrong. Your body should look like this. If we've made you feel bad enough about yourself, here, this product can solve the problem we've just determined to exist in you.

Possible inward stories: My body doesn't look like that. Something must be wrong with me. I hate my body. I wish it looked like that. Their life seems so much better than mine. And hey, they are smiling, I want to smile like that. Maybe that product does work. Maybe that will solve my problems. Maybe I will buy it.

Example 2

Projected stimulus: Anything related to Africa or another place that is presented as desperate to survive.

Intended message: Look at this horrible life being lived. Yours is so much better, make sure you remember that. Feel bad, that's it, feel bad about having all you have whilst sitting on your couch as little babies die with swollen bellies and flies in their eyes. Now, all of this guilt we've stirred up in you, we're going to give you a quick fix, we're going to let you believe you can fix the problem we've just presented to you. Please give us your money now, no, not once off, that's not good enough, monthly forever please... because, *mwahahahahaaa*, try cancelling a charity subscription for sick and dying children.
Note: Please just Google, 'Haiti missing charity money,' for a well-explored example of corruption.

Possible inward stories: Oh wow, how sad, I might even cry today. That poor baby, I can't imagine losing my own. Oh, it's only £3 a month, that's nothing. *Click. Click. Click.* Oh, that's better, at least I'll be helping in some small way. Now, let me make that cup of tea before Love Island comes back on.

Another Note: Other people's 'that's nothing' amounts to a lot; again, please read up on, 'Haiti missing charity money.'

Advice: Please stop watching *Love Island* or anything closely related to it, nothing but bad can come from sexed-up insecure adults playing at porn. I don't judge the people that go on it, far from it, I feel for their vulnerable desperation to be seen, heard and valued in a world that never taught them how to be. Who I do uncharacteristically judge are the people who design and make platforms that take advantage of others on account of their own greed.

I won't go into anymore, the point is, you are stupid, in the sense that your mind doesn't easily discern truth and reality from lie and illusion. And no wonder, from a young age the main reason many of us are given in support of something's truth is, 'Because I said so,' thus it goes on to make sense that we would do the same as adults. I remember this horrible fashion trend that emerged about fifteen years ago, the puffball skirt, unflattering, ill-fitting and just downright ugly. Shock. Shock is what overcame me as I went out on the town and I kid you not, over 50% of the young girls were wearing them. The only reason I ever found for this phenomenon that occurred throughout one eye-sore of a summer was that the magazines told these girls to do it, so they did.

Before now, I have wondered whether the fashion gurus of the world throw out a yearly wild card, a playful dud that they watch mindless shoppers run to buy. I wonder if they sit and bask in their almighty power laughing at it all. I hope not, but this world is home to all sorts and my mind is not entirely happy with the puffball skirt's creation, let alone its success. Scarier still was the summer that skeletons walked the streets, when All Hallows Eve came with great preparation as girls starved themselves to present as the army of the dead, some young men even saw fit to join in too.

Nothing presented to us as real, is real.

There are so many ways of living represented on television, yet to every corner of the earth I have wandered, I have yet to see any one version of reality presented to me as even remotely real. False expectations of hope and delusions of fantasy are what we grow up on. Let's take romance, despite having had been single for over a decade I am a romantic at heart, well, I used to be. What is romance but stories about how love should be? Rather than romance I'd take thoughtfulness any day, although I think ultimately that's what romance is. I, for example, would not appreciate chocolates or dying flowers so much as I would a coupon for a massage or a new lemon tree for the garden. Lived experiences are what I'm after, shared moments of pleasure and joy, not trinkets and presents for the sake of presents.

The ring, two words that can make a lady's heart flutter and a man's palms sweat. I never really grew up fantasizing about a proposal and a white wedding, my mind was more focused on booking flights and exploring new places. But as one begins to age one does start to ponder these things. Sometimes I am frustrated by the mind's inability to unknow a thing, like un-read Harry Potter and read it fresh once again, or re-watch Avatar in 3D for the first time. In this instance, my mind grapples with things like blood diamonds, the advertising of Tiffany & Co. in the 1940s which spawned the popular concept of the engagement ring, and then there's the whole symbolic notion of belonging to another, something quite impossible. At most, for me, a ring symbolizes a promise to try one's best to uphold other promises. The only promise I needed to hear from my man was, 'I promise to own my stuff.'

Promises are all well and good, but action is what makes for results, actions like effective and constructive communication; honest, internal reflection; and an ability to adapt and change. One can promise the world to another, but only if they have a world to give, which most of us don't.

THE ILLUSION OF CHOICE

All of these promises come full of intent and expectation, two things bound to leave you disappointed. Anyone I know in a happy marriage has worked at it, or rather, they worked at their own happiness and learned how to share it. Far too often love is seen as the band-aid of life, the solution to solve all problems, the necessity to your very completion, what codswallop.

I blame popular culture for this, film, series and song, throw some new-age literature in there too. Media sources tell us what love looks like, and this has become our main reference point for something so profoundly life-impacting. Do we look to these sources because there is a lack of observable love around us in society? Do we look here because the alternative, otherwise known as reality, is too difficult to bear? Is love ever really love, or simply a need fulfilled? Real love, is it not unconditional in nature, something not known to as many parents as they might like to think? Anytime a condition is attached to love it becomes *conditional*. The word *love* is easily said by anyone, 'I love you,' there, just said it. Do you believe me? No, of course you don't, because love, as a lexical symbol, is attached to a feeling, a state of being, it is not simply a label for attachment. *I accept you*, now that I can say.

For many of us, we sadly misinterpret an unhealthy attachment or fear-based need of another as an intense form of love. If love were the primary essence of a connection it would be full of harmony, peace and grace, of course there would be conflict, but that of a healthy nature, that which challenges and transforms. No fingers are pointed in love, no tarnishing of blame, jealousy and doubt. There is ultimate trust in yourself as opposed to the other, a trust that you are already whole and complete as you are. My happiness is my responsibility, I have come to terms with this aspect of my reality. And if my own happiness is my responsibility, so too must be my suffering.

Is it fair of me to blame a potential partner for my own living insecurities? Is it okay for any arising jealousy to be thrown at another and determined as their fault? My reaction is mine, no one else's. An external event may trigger it, but all this does is show me it's there, what I must start asking is, where did it come from? This reaction was not born and created in that moment, rather, it quite likely comes from a lack of love in childhood, a void that left fear in its wake, fear of love coming and then disappearing, fear of it never being real, fear of it never happening at all. The tragedy is that the somewhat unsavoury patterns that play out as a side-effect of this internal lack are the very things that create the constant reinforcement of it. The jealous outbursts and panicked rambles are misunderstood by the person living them, as well as by the recipient of the reaction, who probably lived a whole bunch of their own reactions too.

No one chooses to be jealous and insecure, just as no one chooses to be paranoid, possessive or controlling. It's okay to be these things, it's not your fault, you didn't choose to be what you are. I can only be what I am too and sometimes it's hard being me, just as being you comes with its challenges, I'm sure. The brave thing to do is to admit to it and learn to accept and celebrate the colourful human that you are and be bold enough to allow change. I do not advocate the changing of oneself here, it is a person's awareness that must first change, the rest seems to take care of itself somehow.

CHAPTER 14

Be Aware, Be Very Aware!

Ah, that Swiss fellow, Silvio, would enjoy this: be aware > beware. The magic of words. Beware of yourself folks, you live accompanied by both your greatest enemy and greatest ally, your own mind. Becoming aware of yourself is about getting to know your mind, the thoughts it thinks, reactions it has and things it imagines. All these features of yourself present nuggets of contemplation, lived moments that reveal something deeper about yourself. Are you brave enough to look? I find it a funny thought to consider that when we hide from ourselves, when we bury our discomfort at a thing arising within us, all we are doing is ensuring that it stays there. I refer to the stuff happening inside of you with loose terms, like, 'A thing arising,' because the looser the term the better when we are talking about The Self; give that machine a new story to believe in and it will run like the wind with it.

No, this is more about breaking down stories, as opposed to creating new ones. Or rather, it is about becoming aware of the stories that confine us to living in cycles and loops inherited from our ancestors. Stories confine everything in existence, we live our lives in narrative from the moment we can listen, comprehend, speak and make sense. We spend our young lives building a lexical library in our minds, words and meanings forever attached together and used to build a shared existence with others of our species. How amazing humans are, just think of all our wonderfully different languages that evolved around the world. What a miraculous imagining to take a moment and allow the mind to scan the earth over time and watch various civilisations develop their own tongue and then find ways to represent it in print or pictorial form.

I said earlier that we are stupid, let me now counter that with, we are pretty darn clever too and our potential for growth and change seem somewhat limitless.

Can we turn what has become our kryptonite into our collective superpower, thus turning the tides of change in a more mindful direction? We know we can change, history tells us so, can we be the first generation to do so mindfully and peacefully? Can we collectively identify and choose with deliberation the ways in which we need to transform and let this be informed by relevant and up-to-date knowledge? Can we let go of our own stories enough to let the children of the future learn and absorb, 'The New?' Can we allow ourselves to live in a state of fear as we trust the young to carve their own path, empowered with a *knowing of thy self* and tools for life in a new world? Can we let them know better by teaching them to do so? Can we relinquish the power found in rightness and find the humility and honour discovered in admitting we are almost definitely wrong? Can we let them be free of the fear that confines us and become the generation that saves the world rather than destroys it?

Awareness of one's own self and how it works is the key to freedom, and if it is a free world that we seek then it seems logical to identify the starting point of that endeavour as each individual. What do I mean by a free world? I refer to a world free from the internal struggles and conflicts of the mind, for it is the only way to bring the same state into existence externally—as within, so without. The inner and outer worlds are one, delicately intertwined beyond comprehension or recognition. Something happens inside of you, you project it out into the world somehow (movement, speech, drawing, writing), then the world

FAITH

reflects back to you exactly what you expect. When it's not what you expect, an adult form of a toddler tantrum might occur, a rant, ramble, complaint, judgement or conflict. When the world doesn't give us what we want or expect, we return to our default coping mechanisms gifted to us in childhood.

What does your tantrum look like? Do you have one dominant reaction or switch between a few? Do you cry when faced with power struggles and shrink yourself to survive? Do you rage beyond reason and trigger a problem to only get bigger? Do you passively accept everything as a defeat and simply simmer inside? What did life teach you, to kick and scream to get what you want? Or that you'll get nothing you want anyway, so it's better to complain about it rather than take the two options available: accept the thing and stop talking about it or change the thing? One of the most fascinating characteristics of humans, and I'll say it, most annoying also, is their tendency to repeat the same complaint over and over. Teachers are fabulous at this, spending years complaining about the state of affairs and how things need to change. Man, oh man, give it up folks, that thing you're complaining about is reality.

Free yourself from the pain and burden
of wishing reality was different.

BE AWARE, BE VERY AWARE!

I once attended a two-hour English teacher conference, two hours spent listening to how great we all were, what fabulous statistics were achieved the year before and how excited we all are about next year's numbers. This was okay, quite bearable in fact, I knew what to expect, I'd heard it twice before, and more importantly, I knew not to take a moment of it seriously. Not a word was going to impact the work I did with my class the following day. Afterwards, a small group of us congregated at a friend's place, the best reason for work meetings being the happy social that always followed. But by crikey, do you know what happened, half the party, the female half, went on to dissect and discuss said two-hour meeting for a further three hours. That bearable conference quickly turned into torture and I had to shift myself into the company of the gentlemen.

I have come to ponder why it is that I prefer the company of males, it's always been my way. I am not a tomboy, never have been, and I'm not exactly masculine. I have come to consider that our connection comes from our similar state of numbness that occurs as a reaction to particular external stimuli. When it comes to sex, that was always an emotionless experience for me and there had to be an immense physical attraction to pull me forth from my hiding place. There was a definite attachment to whatever charismatic arrogance emitted from my type, as I was drawn to an external persona of confidence. I think maybe these were the only men who could work with my level of non-reaction, those with a delusional level of self-assurance. The first-time emotion and physical intimacy intertwined all hell broke loose, I know what men are running from ladies, and it isn't pretty or easy.

We (me and some men) are running from feelings, internal arisings and happenings that are unidentifiable by our systems and therefore, deemed as dangerous.

The urge to run from love is nonsensical, yet people do it all the time. What they might not realise, in their reactive and confused state, is that they are only ever running from themselves. Facing yourself is hard and something only achievable with a good friend beside you, someone to listen and let you be broken for a while. Phillip did this for me, in a world of lived despair and loss, he was the friend that listened. Others projected their own thoughts and feelings about it all, hollow thoughtless advice, personal comparisons and horror stories of their own. What these people didn't realise, in all of their fixing, was that the only thing their talking revealed to me was that they had work to do too, they just didn't realise it, or chose not to.

I get the not looking at yourself, scars run deep and the

buried pain can be debilitating once dug up. I was crippled for a time, struggling to function and fulfil my basic needs on account of digging up enough of my past to bury myself with it. Years, that's what you're looking at if you choose to commit to yourself, or better yet, a lifetime. The journey with yourself has no end, not until death, and maybe not even then, who knows right? And I think I will only be able to share my life with someone who carries themselves, I can't carry anyone else, not if I intend to live well and become the best mother I can be. As much as I wish for community, I am not one for communal living, nor am I likely to sign up for too many activities or social get-togethers. I am particular about the company I keep and it is a rare few who know me in all my variety. *Complex*, I've been called by some, *intense* by others, but I never feel much like either of those things.

Mostly, I've spent a lot of time feeling tired and wishing for change. I've tried for change, believe me, but it's a tough nut to crack. We really are programmed in the most complex of ways and I think that once it's done, be it by two or five years old, the theories vary, you will be hard pushed to change anything too drastic about yourself. I recently taught a class of six-to-seven-year-olds and I think even by then it might be too late, at least without the development of some revolutionary intervention. I came across stubborn programming, hard-wired tiny humans already full of impulsively displayed patterns of thought and behaviour. Moreover, I was a part of a system ill-equipped to fill the vast majority of individual needs. There is one thing I know can help a tiny individual and that's feeling safe and loved enough to feel their own feelings, whatever they might be, but safe our children are not.

I had to restrain a child some time ago, it is a horrific experience to live, to pin a child to your body for their own safety and for that of the other children. As this tiny animal entered an intense state of fight or flight, only terror was seen by my eyes. Later, we breathed like dragons, I thought it best to simply breathe together, breathing is magic, and what else could we do? God forbid I hug them, I might lose my job, besides, they flinched at touch, even at a gentle hand on the shoulder.

We went on to talk about sweet things as this little person came back to themselves, I watched their body relax as they uncurled themselves from the corner of the room and started to feel safe again. What a devastating thing to witness, I felt every single moment of it: anger at the system that forces this poor child into circumstances they cannot manage; disbelief that this had been allowed to happen for a year; and incredulity at listening to teachers talk with such scorn and distain about a child living in a perpetual state of triggering, without the tools to manage it.

People think they understand children, they don't. They might understand how to control them, oppress them, programme and placate them, but they don't understand children because they have forgotten what it is to be one. Do we bury the memories of our childhoods because the loss of them is too great to acknowledge out loud? Wasn't it really ourselves we lost anyway? Do we live our adult years searching for a feeling we once knew but that disappeared into the land of the forgotten? Do we yearn for an experience we know we lived but can never seem to replicate, the memory of it living on in our bodies and minds somewhere beyond recognition or comprehension? I do believe that children resemble the answers we're all looking for, what a shame it is that we don't often listen to them.

CHAPTER 15

The Voices of Children

Children are voiceless, they don't know how to speak unless we teach them. Know that and believe it. Did anyone teach you how to communicate well? How to listen to a person speak and think about what they said? How to form a worthy response, perhaps even ask a question and not simply project a thought outward? Did anyone teach you how to identify your feelings, get to grips with why they are there and learn to let them inform any subsequent choices or reactions? Probably not, that's no one's fault though, the dialogue about such things did not exist in mainstream settings.

However, these days you've got parents 'de-schooling' their children, a designed lived process that intends to undo any harm or damage that occurred as a result of institutionalised education, and there is a growing wave of home-school communities. As parents recognise the inadequacies of our education systems and the multifaceted threats they pose to their offspring, there seems to be an increase in resistance. School is sure to do one thing, beat the individuality out of your child, their teachers won't want to, but they get beaten too if they don't. Actually, they get beaten whatever they do, that's why I've come to think that all teachers should just start doing what they want. Of course, professional, theory-informed and reflective practice would be expected, but what if teachers dared to trust themselves with what they know they've lived and experienced with children? What would my chosen profession look like if I were simply allowed to do my job and teach tiny humans from my heart and soul?

Do I dare to dream of the joy found in a classroom without anyone to please but myself and the children? It seems an impossible dream, but it shouldn't be, should it? What are we so scared of that we insist children must sit still, look, listen and regurgitate for the vast majority of their young lives, convinced that this is the answer to some stressful unsolvable problem - *the problem of individuality?* School is a neatly designed experience that results in tiny humans learning to walk silently in straight lines, sit the same way in rows and be condemned and shouted at if they sway from the expected norm. I feel the horror of the moment when a teacher makes a child stand up in assembly for talking, their punishment being the intended shaming of up to three hundred and fifty sets of eyes staring them down, and all for living out a natural impulse and behaviour to talk to their friend.

> *We squash the voices of children,*
> *as opposed to listening to them.*

What makes adults think they are so right about it all, other than the fact that the adults before them thought they were right too, and those before them, and so on and so forth? It's a vicious cycle without an end, unless we become brave enough and self-aware enough to start protecting children from their main source of pain and suffering—*us*. We punish children for being themselves, do you all realise that? From the get-go we tell them that our voices are more important and of higher value; as for theirs, well, their little voices are amusing and almost always wrong. You'd be surprised how many of you puppeteer your children for your own amusement. This brings us back to concepts such as Santa, the Tooth Fairy and the Easter Bunny, all designed to inspire your kid towards cuteness or offer up a handy tool for manipulation. Did you know that the Easter Bunny likely originated in Germany? He was indeed a hare at the birth of the idea, one that evaluated children's behaviour, a bit like Santa.

All stories are tainted with threads of the past, just look at the gruesome origins of fairy tales, with ugly sisters rolled down hills in spiked barrels and cruel birth parents. The concept of the literary 'step-mother' was actually introduced by the Brothers Grimm, the idealised love they had for their own parents prompting them to preserve the sanctity of family. With a switch to parental deaths or absences, evil-step figures were permitted to step forward and rain down with terror. The point is, with everything we know and the library of knowledge accessible to us, why do we continue to blindly accept the present as our choosing? I didn't choose the world to be what it is, heck, I didn't even choose to be English, some might say I did, others would say God chose for me, but who knows becomes that simultaneous question and answer again for me.

Although, when I look at the threads of my own life, the rare and special connections I've been gifted with as I travel, the moments of surprising kindness that changed a day around, the wrong turn that turned into a perfect week, I find it difficult to doubt the hand of something greater in my life. There was this moment, some years ago now, when my doubt was dispelled entirely, for a time at least, until fear slowly crept back in as conflicting experiences were once again lived. I was on a tiny island in Vietnam, when a group of people I'd met a week before in the capital strolled past me as I lay sunning myself on the remote, and still somewhat unknown, tropical sands of Con Dao.

You see, I was at the tail end of an eighteen-month overseas trip that saw me travel through Southeast Asia, before and after working as a nanny in New Zealand for a year; I had just abandoned ship on another dream, saving children in that tiny orphanage in Indonesia, hightailing it out of there after just three months, despite my inner dialogue, which demanded it was unethical of me to leave after so little time. About a week before Con Dao, I was sat upon a different tropical beach, scanning the coastline as giant pinnacles stood erect out of the ocean, quite the dramatic spectacle, feeling rather bored and deflated by it all. This was the *wrong* beach; I knew it because I could *feel* it. That night at dinner someone threw out the word 'Vietnam,' and something in my being pricked at the sound, so upon our return to the hostel I booked a flight for the next day.

That's how I've rolled in life you see, my feet have followed my feeling, and I don't think they've led me wrong yet. They've taken me down paths that led toward dark, depressing and challenging, but also in the direction of light, love and trust.   Accepting life as anything but an uncontrollable roller-coaster that you can't get off is foolish, you're here living this life whether you like it or not, but I think perhaps it can only ever be lived with an equal balance of polarity. What I mean to say is...

> *If you run from the dark,*
> *so too do you run from the light.*
> *Both can only ever be lived in equal measure.*

When you enter the darkness within you are able make way for those spaces to be filled with light. That's how it works. Energetically, we all exist on a scale of vibration and frequency. Haven't we all entered a room and declared some variation of, 'I don't like the vibe of this place'? There are clues in the words we use day to day, vibe, connection, chemistry. This spoken sentence reveals more than just a distaste at a past lived experience, it presents an example of how there can be no apparent reason for your dislike of something, or even your dislike of a person, sometimes the vibe, or *vibrational match*, is simply off. I don't know how it works, I haven't sat and measured it, but I know I've felt it and I'm betting you all have too. Can you explain the various levels of internal happenings that result in a sentence like, 'I don't like the vibe of this place,' being spoken aloud? Are there always specific reasons attached to these thoughts or are they sometimes informed by a sense, a feeling?

I happen to think that everything at any given time is informed by a feeling. Something external happens and impacts you, a physiological sensation or occurrence ripples through your being and results in an internally projected thought or dialogue, which is often further projected outwards as a lived and observable reaction. First there is the external stimulus, be it music, the wind or a television show, which your body receives and processes via the senses, including the somatosensory system which allows for the sense of touch. What a funny thing it is to feel an invisible force such as the wind upon your face and not bask in the spectacle of a cool breeze brushing across your skin. This brings us happily back to babies as the perfect representation of our basic nature, their sensory explorations from birth reveal all that we are.

Energetically, this all makes sense, as a visual experiment that goes on to represent an informed and well-researched model of human behaviour, it ticks all of the boxes. I can see the continuous flow, the back and forth nature of human interaction, a continuous cycle of projection and reflection at work. I feel the sound of music impact my body and make it want to move and I enjoy what happens when I let my body flow freely. I feel anger rise up when certain external stimuli occur, is my anger attached to the energy of the event or the arising and then projected thought? Are they one in the same? These days I am able to see my anger rise within, watch it occur and release it with breathing or visual clearing methods. You are your mind, know that now, the only place the world happens is in your own imagination and your imagination hasn't quite got a pin on reality. It likes to interpret and classify, it likes to reflect on the past to make sense of the present and create projections of the future, it likes to *react*.

The past is the only reference point we have for life.

We are limited by what we know, and when we open up to knowing nothing whatsoever, we immediately lessen those limitations. The mind is a powerful thing, an area of the unknown that science is hungry to investigate and understand. Moreover, there is a plethora of reading surrounding mindfulness, meditation, intention setting and energy work, things becoming harder to deny the integrity of. However, every story told fails to acknowledge one simple thing: the unknown will always remain so, we will never conquer it because it is built around the very illusion that we can know anything true, or of real or great significance. Something is only ever significant because we decide it to be so, doesn't that mean we can reversibly declare that none of it is important and free ourselves from the confines of our own thoughts? To be free of your mind is to be free of illusion and illusion is only ever found in knowing. Haven't we done it before when we dropped the story of the world being flat or the earth being the centre of the universe?

But why do we have to wait for contradictory evidence to dispel a myth, why can't we allow our thinking and reasoning minds to live in a constant state of doubt and gentle curiosity? Because to doubt is to fear and us humans, as a general rule, tend to avoid fear-based activities, with perhaps a few exceptions. However, when you grow up in a state of fear there is one happy consequence, as it was in my case at least, you have the opportunity to throw yourself out there into whatever opportunity arises. My main areas of humanness debilitated by fear have been intimacy and meaningful human connection, yet one aspect of life enhanced by my long-harboured flight response was worldwide travel. Returning home was always a confusing thing for me, I didn't often seem to feel how others felt about it and I sure as heck never missed anyone. Not missing people was not only reserved for family, I have never missed a soul, there is lots of therapy wrapped up in those six words. Apparently, it's swaying from the norm not to miss people.

I did of course love people, a friend actually told me to

read a book once about women who love too much, and I think what he was getting at was that I should reserve a little love for myself. This has always been a difficult thing for me to do, put myself before others, something that can become quite crippling when you seem to be needed so very much. You see, this brings me full circle back to the story I started, when I was sitting on that wrong beach in Thailand two weeks away from returning to the UK, full of fear and trepidation as to whether the new joy I had living inside of me would be maintainable once home. There was plenty of past to trigger me in my old life and I'll be honest, I was nervous. However, I was also still on my adventure and was not about to waste a moment of it.

After booking that flight to Vietnam I journaled the words, 'Something is waiting for me there, I can feel it. I wonder what it is...' Comfort, confirmation and faith were waiting. It was in Ho Chi Minh that I met a group of five travellers, which included two other women named Ana, that made for three Ana's, one of whom was convinced she knew me. Apparently, after some delving, we discovered that we went to the same high school, but she remained convinced there was something more to our connection. Later, on that remote beach in Con Dao, we were surprisingly reunited, and it was three days of the other Ana trying to solve this little puzzle presented to her mind, *how she knew me*, before the right question arose within her to ask. As we sat happily sharing a seafood feast, surrounded by the lively buzz of a group of travellers who had spent a day on the sea, the following conversation ensued...

Her: *Wait! What's your surname?*
Me: *Santuario, my name's Ana Maria Santuario.*
Her: *Oh my god! You're Ella's sister?*

This was an identity I hadn't embodied for a while, *Ella Santuario's sister*, that's how people in the wider world referred to me as a teen. My sister is popular, charismatic, confident, kind and funny, yet she became the unfortunate victim of a grievous bodily assault at the age of fifteen. Intuitively, don't ask me how, but I knew before she even spoke, the words that were coming...

Her: *I was there...*

Other Ana, then went on to tell me her story of that night. I think it was a healing experience for us both, she got to talk, I got to listen and realise I was ready to go home. After witnessing two grievous bodily assaults, Ana went on to work as a doctor, she was also the fiercest lesbian I'd ever met and I was in awe of how she owned herself. There is another young lady that comes to my mind whenever I hear the word *lesbian*, Shannon, one of the bravest young women I've ever encountered. We were never great friends, happy acquaintances who shared an appreciation of learning at best, but one day in the school canteen, we must have been thirteen or fourteen years old, she stood up and declared to the all-girl crowd some variation of, 'I am a lesbian, deal with it!' What an absolute rock star! How fearless and self-accepting one must be to do that. How safe in their body and mind?

Anyway, the point this brings me to is, or rather the unanswered questions it all leads to are: what on earth pricked my attention at the word *Vietnam*, enough to make me rather instantly book a flight there? What inspired me to write the words, 'I wonder what is waiting for me...?' How did I end up booked in the same room as this girl who was insistent that she knew me? Were we reunited on that beach simply because we needed to solve this puzzle together? Would we have still met again if we figured it out beforehand in Ho Chi Minh? Or were we always destined to sit on that beach together and let some things go? These are questions with no answers, I could of course make things up and tell you some stories, but there are enough of those around. I'd rather say that what led me to that shared moment in life was a trust in my own intuition.

THE VOICES OF CHILDREN

Every beautiful thing has come from trusting myself.

When I mistrust myself, I live in a state of fear and life becomes stubborn and stuck. Without change, which can only occur with an element of trust, I suffocate and suffer, I don't know why. Do we all? Aren't children the same, increasingly bored of activities, growing and evolving beyond them, only to stop and stagnate at adulthood, unless they are lucky enough to be an expansive person who has learned to live well? Do we really wish to condemn children to live as our own reflections? Are we really so scared of letting them learn to trust themselves and become something different? Can we now trust them to learn all that is new and beyond us, to be programmed in fresh and updated ways and live as better humans than us?

Can we use our intelligence to stop creating more stuff and create a better world by focusing on how to create better humans? By better, I simply mean humans who can learn to live in harmony with the physical environment, as well as with one another. As a teacher, I watch patterns of conflict evolve early on the playground, as children fail to manage their own reactions or even realise that they are having one. They can be hurt by a dodgy look thrown their way or by someone rejecting their friendship; many children, especially boys, display physical impulse issues attached to unidentified and unmanaged anger. But not one single thing is being done to help any of these children learn how to manage their little life. I feel like helping children to understand themselves and how they work is a key to unlocking healthy young humans, another key being *listening to them*.

We really do tell children too much about things, better to let their little minds wander and explore possibility with well-informed intrigue, rather than squash the rainbow of life into tidy little black-and-white boxes, with perhaps a few greys thrown into the mix. Children see the world through eyes that we rip out! Children learn to judge when they learn to believe things, things only we teach them. Children learn to fight only when they have perceived and absorbed this experience as a means to reliving it. Children only ever mirror and mimic, everything they do or say they got from somewhere. Like a little computer they are programmed with words, gestures, behaviour patterns and habits. You know, I never tell a child off for swearing because I know exactly where it comes from, the adult world, why should they be the ones blamed and reprimanded?

Usually we'll have a little chat, something along the lines of, 'I know you might hear adults say that word, but usually children don't. Now I'm not going to tell you off, but if another adult hears you, they likely will. So, it's probably better not to say it again.' I just try to help them out and realise that they can help themselves by not saying the word; after all, it's not their fault that adults can be so idiotic and that their default is to scold rather than teach and nurture. I've seen teachers hand over the news to parents, who then might instil a second punishment later on, therefore prolonging the shame of a lived moment into an entire afternoon, which is perhaps even followed up with a detention the next day. These kids are five to seven by the way, so as a general rule I let swearing slide, usually because the bigger the deal you make of it at that age the more likely it is to happen again anyway; it is *your* reaction that determines whether a child's patterns of behaviour continue or not.

Your child's wellbeing and development are no one's responsibility but your own and all a child's behaviour is ever doing is communicating a need unmet, just like it did as an infant, just as it does for us adults. It's just, and let's be frank, as a species we suck at identifying and communicating our needs, so no wonder children do too. Perhaps we don't need to learn and teach, so much as shut up, observe, think and listen.

CHAPTER 16

What Do They Say?

Listening to children is one thing, interpreting what they say is another. Every lived reaction of a child reveals something deeper at work, we just have to get better at reading the signs. The child who cries every time they lose a game has issues with their own value and self-worth. The one that clings to mum every morning before school suffers from unhealthy attachment anxieties, or they hate the place and are scared of going in. The self-punishing perfectionist who lives with an eraser in their hand and is afraid of mistakes, risk taking, and failure, is already enveloped by fear. And then there's the poor little mite who feels so unsafe that their body and mind have seen fit to shut down their urge to talk, something we refer to in the education system as *selective mutism*. There are infinite ways that unhealthy patterns can manifest, but at the core of each behaviour is a lack of mental, emotional and physical safety.

A child's blueprint for life is as clear as day from an early age and it would be easy to make predictions based on what I see in the classroom. Would it not be reasonable to assume that the little boy with anger issues at the age of seven will display similar patterns of behaviour as a teen and then later as a man? That is unless he receives some kind of intervention to support the development of self-regulation techniques and is directed toward positive change for the long term. Special Educational Needs are widely recognised, Special Emotional Needs are not, perhaps because as a world we seem so scared of emotion and what unlocking it truly means... *change*. For millennia we have been ruled by logic and reason, to an extent we had to be, survival demanded it. But the modern world poses new threats which demand a new defence strategy, this is a war we cannot think our way toward winning, it is one that demands us to step up and add feeling into the mix.

Communication communicates so much more than we realise, my past declarations of being the ultimate independent woman in need of no one smothered an isolated and disconnected existence. Our carefree and thoughtless expressions reveal what's hidden beneath our surface. There's the person scared of commitment who, beneath it all, simply feels unworthy of love. The workaholic who is scared to stop for fear of reality toppling in and the truth of their unhappiness having space to surface for even a second. The egomaniac who has to blow their own trumpet and fake a love for themselves that the world has never shown them. Beneath every story there is space for compassion, behind every unsavoury pattern of behaviour there is a little child whose needs went unmet somehow.

It is easier to cast blame and point the finger, it is easier to be hurt and react than to stop and think about these things. But to not think about these things is to deny children of their right to a comprehension of themselves and a development of self-awareness and self-acceptance, all necessities if they are to survive this world they are born to. Just because we were perhaps not taught to human properly does not mean we should not endeavour to provide our children with the best chance they have at a happy, expansive, full and connected life. Knowledge is power, this has been proven enough throughout time, and if we are to help the children of the future find a manageable and fulfilling path through this maze of a world we have created, well, we need to start equipping them with the necessary tools to do so.

> *One hundred years ago a lack of self-love*
> *and a feeling of ugliness was not fed on*

FAITH

> *and exacerbated by the external world*
> *to such an extent that people were*
> *changing their faces with surgery*
> *and injecting toxins into their tissues.*

The only reason people do it is because the offer is there to do so and the greed that fuels the cosmetics industry has no problem in identifying non-existent problems as real ones: a circle drawn around cellulite, an arrow directed at a pimple, the shaming of a belly roll protruding over denim jeans. It is with contradictory stories that we will help children find their own way to the truth of themselves, with knowledge that celebrates who and what they are, and which nurtures a sense of acceptance and understanding. Those first pimples, for example, I wonder would the shame be so great if teenagers had been raised to know that a pimple reveals a potential imbalance in your body, perhaps nutritional or energetic.

By an *energetic* imbalance, I mean to say that the body presents us with information telling us that something is wrong, a spot is a simple message from the body that can prompt one to ask: Am I sleeping enough? Am I too stressed? What food have I been eating? If it is a strong hormonal reaction that is occurring, is there a nutritional factor that exacerbates the condition? Or are the physical symptoms a sign of something more emotionally underlining, the body's way of releasing unprocessed and repressed emotion that is stored within? Different people have various physical tells, symptoms and signals that their body sends to let them know to sit up and take notice. Perhaps an irritable bowel appears when familial responsibilities surface, or heart palpitations wake you up at night as you repeatedly work to meet deadlines, maybe it's simply an overall lethargy and lack of will to do anything that consumes you.

More than you could imagine, food holds the power to heal you and it is indeed the greatest poison *and* medicine available to humankind. Far too many illnesses that are present in the world today did not even exist before we created them. As a general rule, ill-health presents a sign that there is an imbalance of some kind, be it internal or external, for we've long established that they are one in the same. Too much toxicity results in illness, causes refer to things ingested, inhaled or absorbed from the environment in excess, or beyond the body's ability to self-regulate, process and release. For example, too many unhealthy fats result in clogged arteries and possible weight gain, ingest too much sugar and you might be looking at diabetes, smoke and you compromise your respiratory system. The point is, what is the grandest and most powerful weapon that we can arm children with in this era of exposed and celebrated poor health? Knowledge, that's the only thing.

I'd like to amend the words of a quote from Nelson Mandela, a man of change who I don't think would mind...

> *[Knowledge] is the most powerful weapon which you can use to change the world.*

I think this is possibly what he meant when he referred to education as being the most powerful weapon available to inspire visible change. But the problem is, so long as the knowledge delivered within education systems remains constrained by outdated, fear-based, know-it-all mind sets, our children have no chance whatsoever. We are crippling them for life as these kids waste time regurgitating the same useless rubbish we were taught to regurgitate; the main difference now is that the government upped their game and children are expected to regurgitate more than before. Algebra is a thing before the age of ten and a child must be a proficient poet by seven years old. The world is mad, let's face it. Why are we doing this to children for any other reason than we don't know another way? That was a valid excuse two decades ago, but not any longer, the research speaks for itself and it is time for the powers that be to listen. Perhaps they will when enough of us demand the same thing

— *change*, and perhaps it starts with our children.

First thing I'd advocate for is the building of new schools and the halving of class sizes, any little community over fifteen and it becomes an ongoing process of crowd management, as opposed to an enriched, targeted and individualised learning experience. Then I'd burn every single document related to curriculums worldwide, I'd burn them to ash and then sprinkle said ash into the ocean, thus ensuring the remnants never again be found. Following that, I'd allow our teachers to heal and rediscover themselves, to re-explore what it means to be creative and trust your intuition as you remember what it's like to glide through a day of beautiful teaching and learning. The final thing would be to identify the *actual needs* of these children and design fabulous learning experiences that prepare them for a life lived well in a world that does very little to help them do so.

There are television shows dedicated to ridiculing, yet at the same time popularising, incredibly controversial and unhealthy behaviours and patterns, with no thought as to how it might affect the minds of the vulnerable. We have a responsibility to acknowledge that if something is not good for our children then it is probably not good for us either, a fact that likely contributes to our patterns of avoidance and denial. As children mirror the truth of our unhealthy selves back to us it's far easier to ignore it, rather than do the hard thing and face it head on.

There are of course measured risks we can take, experiences beyond the boundaries of childhood made available to us because we can approach them with rational thought and maintain a sense of internal and external safety, maybe. But the reality is, if you binge drink, if you intoxicate yourself beyond what is safe or manageable for you, well my love, you've got issues to look at. Things we deem as normal in society are absolutely unhealthy. Lifestyles presented on T.V. inspire a distaste of reality, and an appreciation of fantasy and escapism that people mindlessly absorb and imitate.

No one knows what is real anymore, time was you'd be programmed by a small community of humans around you and it was quite a simple thing to develop an identity, sense of self and belonging. But in this ever-confusing world that tells you so much of what's wrong, with no way to make a thing right, doesn't it become less surprising to ponder those poor lost souls who, with so little connection to themselves, use plastic surgery to make their face resemble that of a feline? They were born to a world that had no place for them, identity confusion is an ever-increasing phenomenon that presents in ever-evolving ways and the people who make money off of other people's pain are abhorrent. It is with awareness that advertising campaigns target your weaknesses and plan an assault on your self-esteem and confidence, it goes with the job.

Just think back to those smoking advertisements that once glamorised one of the leading causes of lung cancer, or the popularity of McDonald's and other fast food chains who are shockingly still allowed to target children in their advertising campaigns. Without these things reaching our awareness they will never reach children's, and they must reach children's if they are to survive the world they will be inheriting. We are clueless, let's face it, the world evolved beyond our comprehension and it is increasingly difficult to create a collective story that holds us as a humanity together. The stories of old don't fit anymore, stories have always been there as a way of making sense of the world, they upheld morals and represented the core values of society. These days the stories we absorb contain excessive amounts of violence, sex and casual use of intoxicants, as well as skewed morals and questionable choices matched with unrealistic consequences.

I don't think story-telling time around a burning fire consisted of tales about murder, vengeance, and sexual exploration or exploitation. The same stories were heard by adults and children, for both were expected to uphold the values of community, family and ancestry. The stories that stood the test of time would have been tales that inspired a collective sense of togetherness and survival, they were presented with purpose and for ponderance. Far removed are we from comforting and inspiring folk tales and legends, the era of the individual is here and there is no quick way of going back in the direction of community. We have moved far from the path of togetherness, all walking lost in our own maze of illusion, vastly disconnected from the world and rarely found with a meaningful place to stand in it.

Without being born to community how are we to teach the tiny humans what it looks like, or allow them to know what it feels like to be a part of one? School is where it starts and pending *The Educational Revolution* (watch this space), it is left up to the parents for now. As a teacher my hands are tied, I do what I can, talk about choices and feelings and how to develop your own radar and emotional gauge, I try to help create and sustain days full of happiness. It works you know, I've seen tiny communities transform and strengthen as they explore the concepts of empathy, compassion and understanding, as they learn to see the other person as well as themselves. Talking and listening is all it takes, but amidst all the writing, recording and evidencing there is little time for it.

Parents also work within their own constraints, I am well aware, but that's exactly my point, kids went from being raised by a community, to a mum, to no one, or perhaps by technology. And now, with two-parent working families increasing as the world inflates beyond reasonable living standards, the finger in the hole of the sinking ship of society is the education force. They are the ones punished with the impossible, changing children, that or keeping them the same as they've always been in a world that doesn't allow for it, I'm never quite sure. But we've got it backwards, kids already changed, it's us that need to catch up. Ever had a kid run circles around you with technology or solve a puzzle you couldn't? It's in their blood. It is during the early years that the core of your development as a human occurs; with that said, the youth of today developed differently compared to us and everything about them will be different because of it.

> *The butterfly effect of a million butterflies*
> *is what we are living with.*

There is no easy way out of all this, it's going to take some brutal honesty and brave decisions on our part as responsible adults. The days of walking around with our heads in the sand have to end, you're a standing target that way, just as your children will be, should you fail to face reality. You cannot know everything, it's an impossibility, much better to admit to knowing nothing and start from the

FAITH

very beginning...

CHAPTER 17

The Basic Needs

Towards the beginning of this book, we touched on basic needs and how if you are able to fulfil them at will then you might come to consider yourself lucky, for not all people born to this earth are so fortunate. Gratitude is a good seed to plant from a young age, an appreciation of food and where it comes from, a wonder at how ingested energy transforms into physical energy. And then there's the miracle of breathing and our undeniable connection with nature. Our physiology is fascinating, for a girl there is the wonder of her own body working in lunar cycles, for a boy, his involuntary visible arousal as a response to external stimuli. We are so ashamed of and confused by our bodies, but perhaps with a learned appreciation of them this can start to change. Then there is the home, so desperate are we to fill it with trinkets and treasures, that we forget the

FAITH

blessing it provides during harsh, cold winters or torrential tropical storms.

Our needs became too easy to meet, when did that first happen? Can it be traced back to the human condition of greed, something quite easily dispelled by gratitude? Is it our need and want of more which prevents us from discovering the gifts found only in the present? Is it the stories we are delivered and told that result in the chronic state of unhappiness and conflict that the world finds itself existing in? Does world peace begin with each person learning what it means to become peaceful within themselves? If it is our nature to mirror and mimic, how are we to break the cycles of pain and suffering that have kept the world entrenched for millennia?

The world is getting smaller and wars are getting bigger, wars beyond my comprehension or pay grade. Has any modern war ever been fought without some hidden motive of money or power? I think it unlikely, but it is only ever going to be something for the historians of the future to uncover, as all involved with said horrors dwindle and die. Conspiracy theories are not my puzzle to solve, but the reality of their potential existence is definitely mine to ponder, the world is not what you think it is folks. I can't tell you what it is, I certainly don't know, but I might know some of the things it is not. The world is not kind or nurturing, not the world humankind made anyway, it is not compassionate and truly does not care who you are or what happens to you.

If you are lucky you might have a few people who would mourn your death beyond a year, but we all know that filling a hand of fingers with a list of good, trustworthy and reliable friends is no easy feat. I think that when we are trying to fill those fingers up with friends, what we are really wishing for is family, an extension of the community we were born to, which is perhaps why so many are left continuously hurt and disappointed. As people cyclically fail to meet unrealistic expectations left over from needs unmet throughout childhood, people's social circles get smaller and smaller over time. Do you notice that it is a rare person who expands into various social circles as an adult? Most of us find a tribe and commit to it, comfortable and familiar as it is.

I once had a happy fantasy about friendship, I was in New Zealand when I envisioned two young girls, larger than life characters with bleached hair, fake tans and pink nails, accompanied by loud screechy voices, living a moment of consolation:

Luscha: *Hey Nat! You're not gonna believe it, that guy over there just said I'm intense!*

Natalie: *What the actual, Lusch, no way are you intense. You're amazing girl. I love ya!*
Luscha: *Na sis, you're totally right. What a dick! Love you too, now let's go dancing!*

A perfect example of mirroring and how the people you keep around you happily confirm the reality you find yourself believing in. Communities revolve around belief and shared values, and they are intrinsic to shaping and sustaining the shared world that we live in. But with so many conflicting stories in existence how are any of us to know what to believe in these days? With a matrix of information accessible at our fingertips, where do we begin? With our basic needs is the answer.

If there is any one thing that you do well after reading this book, let it be learning to take care of the vessel that is your home for life, your body. It's where your mind lives as well as your physical organs and it seems logical to assert that it is all connected somehow. You are energy, food is energy, the food you eat becomes you, thus it becomes the energy you utilise and exert. But the world has it all topsy-turvy and has lost its sacred connection of oneness. The Harvest Festival has become nothing more than a token of remembrance, even in the jungles of Borneo it has turned into a royal piss-up! But food represents our connection with nature and the eternal cycle of transformation ever present in our own being.

*If mother nature is the tree,
then we are her fruit.*

The simplest place to look for the answers we seek is to the natural world. We seem to think we are different to other animals, so much so that we make up entire stories about it all, we even spend time debating whether or not we should eat them. Look, other animals eat animals, I don't see that there should be any one singular rule, but many of those who advocate a vegan lifestyle do so from an ethical standpoint that acknowledges our connectedness. I became a vegan once and was met with so much fear from others it was unbelievable. Their fears manifested as loaded questions and conflict, I never once hopped on any high horse, I was mostly doing it because I'd met a girl with glowing skin who put it down to her vegan diet. My motivations only increased with further research and the proof found in the pudding, my banging new body.

Yet the observable and experienced changes were not enough to break my stubborn patterns and cycles of poor health and self-care. I have worked as hard as anyone to change for the better, to become the best version of myself I could be, but in doing so I was constantly denying the reality of who I was, someone who found healthy hard. Whenever I wished for different it came from a place of suffering, inspired by self-judgement and critique, rather than being fuelled by compassion and gentleness. The truest words I've ever lived by are:

Slow and steady, be gentle with yourself.

It became my life motto and I've realised we are only ever moving as fast as we're moving, any sense of rushing only exists inside of yourself and can only ever negatively impact an experience. Consider being late for work and driving at an increased speed, you could do so knowing that you will get where you're going as soon as you can, or you might opt to panic, fluster and create a problem where one does not need to exist, all whilst driving at the exact same speed.

Reality is never a problem unless you make it so. The language we use daily is problematic, we habitually partake in chronic cycles of complaint, whereby a point is identified in reality as unwanted, nothing can be changed about it, but apparently it needs to be talked to death about for no apparent reason. We take up issue with things happening in the world beyond our control and spend so much of our valuable time discussing it. Do you know how many other things we could be talking about rather than the news, the latest T.V. shows or politics? There is a big wondrous world out there full of fascination, wonder and intrigue. There is music to be listened to and dances to be danced. There are fresh waters to be swam in and hot sands to fill the gaps between your toes. Why are we wasting our time?

The world has changed but we are still living life like the fearful little settlers who arrived to meet an uncertain future. The future is pretty certain these days guys, if you follow your nose and sniff out the stuff worth listening to and throw away the rest. Eat well and share the pleasure of food and communication, sleep delicious sleeps and enjoy your soft pillow, relish in the hot water filling your bath and enveloping your body with warmness, be grateful for all that you have. Have you ever tried to spend an entire day in gratitude? It's not as easy as it might sound. Perhaps that's what practices such as Lent and Ramadan try to inspire, thanks forced upon a person by the felt absence of a desired thing. More so, maybe that's why we lack gratitude these days, because we want for nothing and have been left with no reference for what it means to live with an appreciation of our basic needs being met.

Bringing the world back to our one commonality seems like a healthy starting point to reconnecting as a species. In water, food and shelter, do we find our way home to one another? Back to love? Is it by stripping away all that is false, all the decorations we have covered ourselves in and stay hidden behind, that we are able to look in the face of another and see ourselves again? I look around and feel little connection to this world or any way of life lived in it. Technology presents a new force in the breakdown of human interaction and connection, and I find the zombie look unappealing. My own passive approach to social media scared me and I abandoned ship six years ago, preferring to choose what enters my mind and body, rather than helplessly absorb it without a second thought.

> *You absorb everything around you at*
> *any given time in some way or another,*
> *you have your sensory system to thank for that.*

Not everything will register consciously, but as an energetic entity it is a scientific certainty that you will be impacted somehow by the sounds, sights, smells and sensations you experience daily. With this in mind, it seems important to start contemplating the energetic frequencies we expose ourselves and our young to, consider your own feelings as the measuring tool for this experiment. Shall we call it an *emotion-meter*? For example, when you get that spike of adrenaline at a car chase, is it not the same lived experience as a child watching their favourite superhero fight bad guys? An artificially stimulated experience is designed in such a way as to evoke particular reactions from you.

Similarly, a sad emotive song combined with projections of light showing two figures saying goodbye to one another might evoke an array of mental reactions and projections, but one similar sequence of physiological feelings and sensations would be lived by all. We are not as different as we like to think, the only thing that makes us different from one another being the thoughts we think. What we believe, the opinions we have, the direction our life takes, are all determined by what we are filled up with energetically since birth. The words we hear become the words we speak, the lessons we learn tend to be the lessons we teach, and the stories we live become the stories we tell. But how many of us are truly living life? How many of us have grabbed this mother by the horns and ridden her into the great unknown?

I wonder if I was an adventurer in a past life, a person with a thirst for the unknown and unpredictability, for monotony would only lead to certain death in my world, a monotony of the mind, not the exterior. Perhaps with everything discoverable by adventure already discovered, with every lone island now known to man, there was no place left for me to roam. And so, as I lost myself to the jungles of Borneo, I somehow managed to find my way home, life forcing me into a circumstance wherein I was left with no option but to venture inside of myself. There was no map for the lands I traversed, no compass to guide me through the stormiest of seas, no survival guide to make it through the harshest of winters. But make it through I did. I think this whole time I was looking for something I lost some time ago, the things I loved doing, I lost sight of them around the time adulthood started intruding on my time and space.

Before the adult world admitted me to its ranks, I would dance, sing and practice yoga daily, nimble as I was you could bend me like a rubber band by the age of seventeen. I battered out any and all frustrations on my drum kit, although that hobby was inspired more by a personal passion as opposed to a need to vent, possibly providing an outlet beyond my awareness at the time though. During my years of adolescence, I engaged in various activities, such as drama, choir clubs, dry slope skiing, knitting, swimming, the gym and just general self-care practices. I've always enjoyed time with myself, giving myself a facial, painting my nails, enjoying a bath sprinkled with lavender or reading a book in the sunshine. The things I loved doing disappeared from my life for a decade, consumed as I was by my pain, I became smothered by my own suffering, trapped by experiences I lived beyond my own choosing. But it was all hidden beneath a smile, one even I believed was real.

There is no way to move beyond pain other than to feel it, the only way is through. We live in a world smothered by a suffering that it simultaneously creates and sustains. Yet unless the world suddenly wakes up tomorrow with a collective new mind set, it seems unlikely to expect adults, en masse, to change anything important anytime soon. The best shot the world has at saving itself is by saving its children. In reality, we need not do much at all, just to stop doing most of the things we do.

CHAPTER 18

Can We Stop Now?

I wonder whether tomorrow you could stop doing all of the things that are unhealthy for you, eating too much sugar, drinking too much beer, watching too much T.V, spending too much time on social media. The recurring theme here is one of *too much*. It is only ever things in excess that pose a problem and threaten our livelihood and sense of wellbeing; balance is another key to a life lived well. But how many of us have tried to break those bad habits? How many of us have succeeded only for them to be replaced by another unhealthy vice? Like I said, we are a stubborn species and many of us are quite beyond change, our capacity for lived change is perhaps one of our greatest aspects of self-denial. In our grandiose image of self, we deny our very nature and well-documented limitations as a species. Simple and complex, I don't know how we can be both things at once,

FAITH

but we are.

It is the stories we believe about ourselves that are most damaging to the world, our egotistical nature allows us to walk through life with a god-like superiority over all in existence, as we slowly eat away at our home, just as a parasite does its host. It is us who destroys forests, it is us who pollutes oceans, rivers and mountainsides, it is us who obliterates other species from the face of the earth. It wasn't me, it probably wasn't you, but it was *us*. As another example, it is clear and apparent that The Apartheid in South Africa was not of my own doing, yet this fact does not excuse me from a responsibility to live life in a way that contradicts every value upheld during that regime. I do not, today, get to sweep aside the fact that I am a part of the whole, that I am either a part of the problem or a part of the solution. We constantly blame others for the world being how it is, but so long as that's our default setting nothing is likely to change, talking about something is very different to doing something about it.

The main problem today is that there are far too many somethings to choose from and picking your cause has become far too personal, the divisions and divides we've introduced with words and slogans are not always helpful. Some fight for LGBT rights, others for racial equality, for others it is a fair and liveable wage they are after. Everyone is fighting their own fight, but the only way we will ever truly win is together. Is it possible to unite all people behind one cause? What is one thing we all have in common? What is the one universal thing in existence that we are all programmed to fight for and defend? Why, children of course. They also have the happy circumstance of presenting as the very viable and reasonable channel of change the world has been waiting for.

We are presented with a choice here, to remain in ignorance, therefore denying our children a chance at saving the planet, or open up their futures by opening up their minds. We know the facts, it's just our minds don't know how to adapt to this new world, we are not capable of presenting the changes the world needs as it continues to evolve beyond us. Adaptable humans are what the world requires, individuals who are programmed to get with the programme, and quick. Our communities are so rooted in fear that it becomes the same thing we entrench children in, it is our collective fears we must free them of, fear of the other, fear of themselves, fear of the world being what it is.

We like to sugar coat things for kids, protect them from the world for as long as possible, but keeping them in ignorance is like preparing a lamb for the slaughter. Arming our children with well-selected knowledge, skills and life-tools is the best thing we can do for them. Believing in Santa does little to prepare your children for the world, better to worry about their twerking the next time it arises rather than when they start questioning the legitimacy of an invisible man. We worry about the wrong things, might we start worrying about the right things, like whether our children are happy, whole inside and physically healthy? Are they still cartwheeling, or did they stop that when the tests at school started? When they sit down to read a book how do they approach it, with excitement and intrigue or a sense of foreboding?

> *If ever a child presents with a problem, whenever their behaviour communicates an imbalance, discomfort or need, it is your job to play detective and figure it out.*

Google can be your best friend when you are discerning and read with intrigue as opposed to fear. It's no good reading to feed an already existent panic, in that case, better to read about your parental anxieties and get a check on yourself. You're allowed to feel them, just stop letting your child feel them too. You are your responsibility to manage, not theirs. Far too often parents say things they shouldn't in front of their children, talking about them like they're not there is the worst offense, an action completely absent of any acknowledgement of their existence. Then there are the adults who keep kids waiting, just because they can. At your mercy, you make them wait until you've finished saying your very boring thing, which to you seemed very important, just as important as their little voice was to them when waiting to express itself.

What is the right thing to do in this situation? Why it all depends on where your child is at in their development. Do they yet have the capacity to recognise the needs of another? Do they have enough awareness beyond the moment to comprehend the value and purpose of manners or a polite interjection? To know your child, you have to know your stuff. There is no roundabout way of saying it, reproducing a child is no sure-fire guarantee to becoming a decent parent and it is necessary to read, learn and reflect, continuously. Personal reflection simply means looking at yourself and relating it to whatever happens as a result of particular actions or decisions. If the way you handle your child results in a tantrum it is no one's fault but your own and it is yourself that you need to look at; the child and their behaviour merely represent symptoms of your own unhealthy choices.

The child is never the problem, only you are. Well, you're not a problem exactly, but you are the factor that needs to shift and change, children literally can't as they lack the capacity to do so independently. Traditionally, children become themselves based on their exposure to external environmental factors and a unique sequence of lived experiences, it is how we all became what we are, just as all humans before us did too. What I begin to question is whether we can deliberately design experiences for children to live in such a way that we deliver on the concept of a healthy human. For the first time in our existence science and spiritualty are meeting meaningfully, and it's making room for change. As neurological research proves the benefits of meditation and mindfulness, the practices are being embraced. As humans become more able to observe and measure the trajectory and impact of energy in motion, the word *energy* demands more acceptance beyond the realms of the hippies.

> *The world changed already,*
> *we just have to allow ourselves to do the same,*
> *and let go of a past that we are wired to hold onto.*

The only thing we're ever really afraid of losing is ourselves anyway, but we are already so lost that it doesn't really matter what we do, our blueprint for life lives in us already, the best we can do is learn to accept ourselves. But the children, now *they* have a fighting chance at a brighter and better future, if only we'd give them the opportunity to find their way to figuring out what that looks like. In the present day we find ourselves inundated with information, with knowledge accessible at the touch of a fingertip we are a click away from answering any question we might have. So, it makes sense that it is the asking of the right questions that leads to the most fruitful experience for the curious human mind.

Can we get children asking the right questions? Some important ones might be, who wrote this, was it researched, how was it evidenced, how old is the link, and is there any truth to it whatsoever? So long as we raise children to mindlessly believe the word of adults, it is how they will continue to live throughout their lives. Critical and divergent thinkers, questioners, fearless pioneers living with relentless reminders of the unknown is what we're after. Time was when the future was fairly certain within a lifetime, predictable in nature and cyclic in event, but now it is a big ball of chaos, which is openly displayed with a repetitive dialogue delivered under an air of importance. Here I am of course referring to the news, that show full of devastating things you must know and talk about incessantly. How boring it all is, do you ever hear one version of devastation and despair that you haven't heard before? Do yourself a favour, switch it off, the news doesn't do anybody any good.

FAITH

I think one of the fundamental mistakes we make is mislabelling what is important. We hold inconsequential topics such as the news in high regard but shirk off a discussion as important as a relationship or the betterment of our health. It's easier to keep looking at the other stuff, it poses a happy distraction, doing the exact job it is designed to do. It is only by identifying that which is unhealthy that we might start to protect our young from it. Is there any reason for them to have an inkling of awareness that the news exists? If they cannot comprehend a concept as complex as distance and even fathom where Iran is on a map, do they need to hear anything about what's happening there? Big fat no!

Just because you think something is important does not mean it's important for your child to know, especially before they are ready. Arm yourself with knowledge, it is your best defence against poor parenting, that and brutal self-honesty. A high-value parent faces their fears, they do not hide behind them. Someone who births a child has the ultimate responsibility of shaping them, and this is a call of the tallest order. I haven't yet met a person qualified to do the job entirely well and I'm sure my involuntary humanness will undoubtedly fudge up my own children somehow, should I have any. What a magical experience it must be to have life grow inside of your own body, and it's one I wholeheartedly hope to have. I may not be able to guarantee what they become, but perhaps I can learn to let them become what they already are, *themselves*.

The only thing that ever gets in the way of a child discovering who they are is an adult, didn't the same thing happen to you? Can we stop it now and learn to allow the next generations of tiny humans to make their own discoveries and carve their own paths toward new and different? Can we catch them up to the present and empower them with the appropriate know-how and tools to survive this crazy ride we call life? Can we let go of enough of ourselves to stop standing in the way of change and accept the reality of what we are, a bunch of animals who believe in some stuff? Can we start choosing what we believe in as we relax a little into a new way of being? Can we, in full acknowledgement of our own nature, come to sustain an allowance of the beliefs and ways of others? Can we stop expecting others to change, and in doing so, accept the nature of the world and our own species? Can we hold faith in ourselves and allow our stories to change, thus letting go of the past to make way for a future that looks a little bit like the unknown?

READY TO DELVE DEEPER?

Visit Anamaria.org for more reading and mirrors of reflection...

To see yourself evermore clearly, and read as the perfect aside to *Faith, In Stories That Change,* Ana Maria Santuario offers part of her debut poetry collection, *A Journey of Subtraction*, for free when you subscribe to her monthly mailing list, but you can also purchase it on her website, as well as from main global book seller websites and in various stores around the world. There are also free resources of self-support being added constantly to The Self-Help Library, found at Anamaria.org, where we invite skilled and experienced light and love workers, or healing experts, to develop with us and add to this feature of the website. All helpful life enhancing learnings are fully funded and delivered with the help of *The Ana Maria Foundation*, a charity that practices love as their main ethos.

A JOURNEY OF SUBTRACTION

A Collection of Poetry and Prose

All who traverse inward require pointers, a compass, so to speak. Let *Subtraction* guide you home, towards the self, through the self, beyond the self. This collection of poetry and prose complement any journey of self-inquiry, whereby the destination lay inwards, through ethereal oceans unknown to the eye. Ana Maria offers mirrors of reality, reflections of compassion and love, and writes with the 'soul' purpose of calling you home.

Available for wholesale purchase from The Ingram Content Group, finer details of contract are available at Anamaria.org:

> ISBN 978-1-8380743-9-5 (hardback)
> ISBN 978-1-8380743-0-2 (paperback)
> ISBN 978-1-8380743-1-9 (ebook)
> ISBN 978-1-8380743-2-6 (large text edition)
> ISBN 978-1-8380743-7-1 (audio book)

www.ingramcontent.com/pod-product-compliance
Lightning Source LLC
LaVergne TN
LVHW021703060526
838200LV00050B/2479